THE Road Guide TO
Yosemite

THE Road Guide TO Yosemite

Bob Roney

Maps and illustrations
by Eric Knight

YOSEMITE CONSERVANCY

Yosemite National Park

YOSEMITE CONSERVANCY.

yosemiteconservancy.org

Library of Congress Control Number: 2012946781

Caveat

Given the rapidity with which things change, the accuracy and completeness of the contents of this book cannot be guaranteed. The names of businesses mentioned here are provided as a service to readers and not as an endorsement or guarantee. In addition, the publisher and the author assume no legal responsibility for the safety of the reader and urge all visitors to Yosemite National Park to obey traffic laws and all safety signs.

Cover photograph: Bob Roney

Cover design: Nancy Austin

Interior design: Nancy Austin

ISBN 978-1-930238-36-7

Printed in China by Everbest Printing Co. through Four Colour Imports, Ltd. Louisville, Kentucky

1 2 3 4 5 6 — 17 16 15 14 13

Photo, page 2: El Capitan from Valley View.

Contents

SYMBOLS USED IN THIS GUIDE

▲ Campground	🪑 Picnic table
🥤 Drinking water	📞 Phone
🍴 Food	🏠 Ranger Station
⛽ Gasoline	🚻 Restroom
ℹ Information	🥾 Trail
🖼 Interpretive Exhibit	🗑 Trash

STANISLAUS NATIONAL FOREST

Tower Peak

YOSEMITE NATIONAL

Cherry Lake

Tuolumne River

Hetch Hetchy Reservoir

Grand Canyon of the Tuolumne River

Hetch Hetchy Road
Page 56

Hetch Hetchy Entrance

Mather

White Wolf

Mt. Hoffmann

May Lake

120

Big Oak Flat Entrance

Tuolumne Grove

Merced Grove

Crane Flat

Yosemite Valley Roads
Page 24

Yosemite Falls

Yosemite Village

Half Dome

Tenaya Canyon

Big Oak Flat Road
Page 48

YOSEMITE VALLEY

Glacier Point

Foresta
Arch Rock Entrance

El Portal

Merced River

140

El Portal Road
Page 42

Badger Pass

Chinquapin

Glacier Point Road
Page 98

Buena

Wawona Road
Page 86

Wawona

Mariposa Grove

South Entrance

SIERRA NATIONAL FOREST

41

0   5 Miles

N

TOIYABE

NATIONAL FOREST

Twin Lakes

Sawtooth Ridge

PARK

Lundy Lake

Mt. Conness

Saddlebag Lake

INYO

Mono Lake

Lee Vining Canyon

Lee Vining

Tioga Road
Page 62

Mt. Dana

Tioga Pass Entrance

NATIONAL

Tuolumne Meadows

Dana Fork

Cathedral Peak

Lyell Fork

Kuna Crest

FOREST

Cathedral Range

Tenaya Lake

Mt. Lyell

Merced River

Mt. Ritter

Clark Range

Ritter Range

Vista Crest

ANSEL ADAMS
WILDERNESS

167

395

120

158

Yosemite National Park

Introduction

Yosemite's roadways have a rich history, providing access to the park's dramatic beauty and containing stories of exploration, discovery, tragedy, and joy.

In fact, Galen Clark, the first guardian of the Yosemite Grant, had roads in Yosemite Valley built before there was even a road to get there. The first carriages were disassembled, hauled in on muleback along early trails to the Valley, and then reassembled. James Hutchings, an early hotelkeeper, drove one of these first carriages. He died, ironically, in a carriage wreck along one of the early roads into Yosemite Valley on Halloween evening of 1902.

Stage drivers and guides provided the earliest roadside information, often inflating facts and figures or making them up altogether. When automobiles took the place of wagons, guides exchanged reins for steering wheels and continued telling stories. In the 1920s, ranger-naturalists often hopped aboard tour cars to extol the wonders of Yosemite and interpret its natural and cultural history. In the 1930s, rangers

In the 1930s, Rangers led auto caravans about Yosemite Valley, making stops to interpret the scenery.

even led caravans of automobiles throughout Yosemite Valley.

In the early days, ranger-naturalists wanted the public to "learn to read the trailside (or roadside) as one would read a book." This road guide has its roots in that philosophy and will help you understand some of the history and natural history along the roadside.

HOW TO USE THIS GUIDE

The tour portion of this book is divided into seven sections: Yosemite Valley and each of the six major roadways in the park: El Portal Road, Big Oak Flat Road, Hetch Hetchy Road, Tioga Road, Wawona Road, and Glacier Point Road. Scenic and historical points on each road are lettered according to the name of the road (e.g., **T** for Tioga Road) and also numbered in sequence, with number 1 closest to Yosemite Valley on each tour. These combinations of letters and numbers can be found throughout the park on marker posts that are placed alongside these roads. This book is keyed to the marker posts that you'll see as you drive along.

All markers have turnouts or parking areas, so please pull completely off

Yosemite's early visitors arrived by horse and carriage. James Hutchings and his wife pause for a photo on Halloween evening, 1902.

the highway when you stop. Also, be mindful that it is dangerous to park facing traffic. Directions and the distance between each point of interest are noted in italicized text.

SERVICES

There are few automobile services or gasoline stations in the park. There is a garage in Yosemite Valley that can handle mechanical problems, and roadside service is available with an AAA card or a credit card. Other companies may respond through the Yosemite Garage in Yosemite Valley: phone (209) 372-8320 or (209) 372-1060. Gasoline is available at Tuolumne Meadows during the summer season and at Crane Flat, El Portal, and Wawona throughout the year. There is NO gasoline in Yosemite Valley. Cell phone service is marginal within Yosemite, Wi-Fi is limited to lodging facilities, and there are few pay phones.

INTERPRETIVE EXHIBITS

Informative interpretive exhibits along roads throughout the park help visitors understand or identify scenery along the way. Some of these exhibits are located in the same places as the stops in this book, and others are not. While many cover the same information in this book, some cover completely different subjects.

An interpretive exhibit near Tioga Pass.

Cars sometimes hit coyotes that run across the road to beg for food.

SPEEDING KILLS WILDLIFE

Every year, cars hit several dozen bears, hundreds of deer, and thousands of smaller animals. You can help save lives by being a more attentive driver and by driving more slowly. Park roads were built for scenery—not speed. You may find areas where the speed limits seem unreasonably slow, but there are good reasons.

Yosemite is a sanctuary for both people and wildlife. Some species are particularly susceptible to death by car because they frequently walk, hop, or fly across roads in the park. Drivers who speed kill many rare or uncommon animals. None of us wants to be in that situation.

THE LIFE YOU SAVE MAY BE YOUR OWN

The most common way people die in Yosemite is in traffic accidents. Driving more slowly and being alert not only reduce injuries and death, they provide for more time to react and avoid hitting something or someone—not to mention making the drive much more comfortable and enjoyable. One purpose of this guide is to show you where you can stop safely in turnouts and parking areas to enjoy the landscape and learn more about its natural and human history.

If you have an emergency, call 911.

Natural and Human History of Yosemite

GEOLOGIC STORY

Billions and billions of years ago, in the deep darkness of time, a great star shone brightly in a young universe. The star itself had existed for billions of years, fabricating helium from hydrogen in its nuclear forge. Other elements, such as oxygen, carbon, and iron, also fused into existence—but no element was more massive than iron. This blazing star would soon signal the end of its existence in a tremendous explosion, and the supernova of that star would eventually lead to the discovery of Yosemite Valley and the creation of national park systems worldwide.

When the star exploded, pieces of it slammed so hard into one another, and at such velocity, that they fused into elements more massive than the star's nuclear fusion alone could produce, such as silver, lead, and gold. Gases and solids alike spewed out into the void, ultimately congregating with the wreckage of other stars. This material would fall together, creating a new star system, which included four rocky planets. The third stony planet out from that star would eventually cool and come to be known as Earth.

Some 4.5 billion years later, some of the heavier elements born in the fiery deaths of stars caught the attention of newcomers to the Sierra. The California gold rush was on, and that would lead to friction with various American Indian tribes, then war, and then the discovery of Yosemite Valley by civilians.

Plate Tectonics and Volcanism

As the hot new planet cooled, lighter rocks solidified and floated on the denser, hotter material below—much like the "skin" that forms on hot pudding as it cools. This skin of rock broke into large pieces geologists call plates.

There are two kinds of plates: continental plates, which float higher on the surface of the globe, and oceanic plates, which float lower. These plates, propelled by slow-moving currents inside the planet, float around the surface, grinding into, under, over,

Opposite: Milky Way over Yosemite.

oceanic plate   continental plate

Tectonic plates on the surface are propelled toward each other by convection currents within the earth

Heavier oceanic plate subducts and melts

Magma rises up into continental crust

Granite forms when pools of magma slowly cool and solidify underground

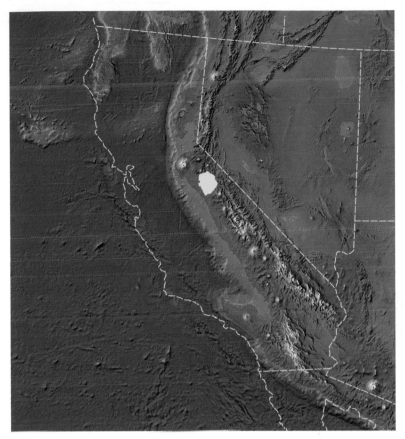
Geographic setting of California around 90 million years ago.

and across one another like flotsam on a sea of semimolten rock.

One of these plates, the Farallon oceanic plate, crashed into the North American continental plate. When a continental plate and an oceanic plate collide, the heavier oceanic plate dives (or subducts) beneath the lighter continental plate. As the Farallon Plate descended beneath the North American Plate, rock began to heat up and melt.

This melted rock, or magma, rose toward the surface. Some of it erupted through volcanoes as lava, forming a volcanic mountain range we call the Ancestral Sierra Nevada. It was located right about where today's Sierra Nevada stands. The Pacific coast was about where the Sierra foothills are today. The magma cooled and solidified as much as three to five miles beneath the surface. Those pools of solidifying magma became the granites we see throughout the modern Sierra Nevada.

Nature is ever at work building and pulling down, creating and destroying, keeping everything whirling and flowing, allowing no rest but in rhythmical motion, chasing everything in endless song out of one beautiful form into another.

JOHN MUIR, *THE YOSEMITE NATIONAL PARK*, 1909

Opposite: Simplified view of Earth's structure showing formation of granite below the ancestral Sierra Nevada.

Glacial Landforms

Cirques are found on many of Yosemite's highest peaks. Accumulating snow compacts into glacial ice and starts to flow downhill, plucking away rocks and scooping out these circular alcoves near the crest.

The **zone of accumulation**, where more snow falls annually than melts.

Debris from **rockfalls** is carried down the glacier, forming **lateral moraines** along its margins.

The **zone of ablation**, where glacial ice gradually melts as it reaches lower elevations.

The bare ice exposed here each summer is pitted and fractured with **crevasses**.

Where tributary glaciers have joined together, their lateral moraines merge to form **medial moraines.**

At its **terminus**, the glacier appears stationary. But the ice is still flowing downhill, melting away as quickly as it advances.

Rocks are released from the melting ice, depositing huge piles of debris around the terminus called **end moraines:**

Recessional moraines outline places where the glacier paused on its retreat.

The glacier terminus advances and retreats as the climate changes.

Terminal moraines outline the farthest extent of the glacier.

Ice melts and **outwash streams** flow from the glacier regardless of whether it is advancing or retreating.

This glacier used to be much larger!

Meltwater often forms **glacial lakes** like this one behind the end moraines left by a retreating glacier.

Many of Yosemite's lakes and meadows originated when glaciers retreated from the landscape during the past 10,000 years.

Uplift and Erosion

Muir's words were never truer. The current state of these beautiful mountains and valleys is only a moment in geological time, in the building up and tearing down of the Sierra Nevada.

Nearly 100 million years ago, the volcanic mountains of the Ancestral Sierra Nevada, similar, perhaps, to the Andes of South America, rose possibly as high as 20,000 feet above sea level. Those mountains are now mostly gone, having been weathered and eroded away.

Two opposing forces shaped the landscapes of Yosemite and the Sierra: uplift, which builds mountains, and erosion, which tears the mountains down.

Rivers of Water, Rivers of Ice

The volcanic landscape of the Ancestral Sierra gave way to a rugged mountain range of granite, which rose as the elements broke down the older mountains and rivers carried them away. Water flowing through the bottoms of granite canyons cut deeper and deeper, leaving them with V-shaped profiles.

During the last 2 million years, glaciers flowed from alcoves near the crests of these new mountains, like deep, slow-moving rivers of ice. They moved down through preexisting river canyons, deepening and widening them into broad U shapes in cross section.

Mountain glaciers begin when snow falls winter after winter without melting completely each summer. Year after year, the snow piles higher and higher until it compresses under its own weight and solid ice forms. When the ice becomes thick enough—about 150 feet thick—it begins to flow downhill, plucking rock from the side of the mountain and scooping out a hollow amphitheater at the head of the glacier called a "cirque."

If you've ever played with Silly Putty, you've seen a similar phenomenon. Leave the lump in its egg, and it oozes into the shape of the bottom of its container, and eventually its top surface flattens out. Glacial ice flows in a similar way. Meltwater also moves glaciers by lubricating the glacier's base, allowing it to slide more easily over the bedrock.

Eventually the ice flows to a lower elevation, where warmer temperatures cause it to melt back as quickly as it moves forward. The glacier appears to be still, but it's not. Like a slow-moving conveyor belt, the glacier carries rock debris embedded inside and on top of the ice and dumps it at its snout.

Geologists call the part of a glacier where the ice is melting back "the zone of ablation," and the area of a glacier where snow and ice accumulates "the zone of accumulation." The accumulation of rock and debris carried and deposited by a glacier is called a "moraine."

When the lower end of a glacier remains in the same place for a while, rock material piles up in what is called an "end moraine." One kind of end moraine marks the farthest extent of the glacier's ice and is called a "terminal moraine." If the glacier recedes and then stops again, it makes another deposit, called a "recessional moraine."

Piles of rock that fall out or off of the glacier to its sides are called "lateral moraines." When two glaciers join, their lateral moraines crush together in the middle of the combined glacier to become a "medial moraine."

A BRIEF HISTORY OF YOSEMITE VALLEY

A. *About 5 million years ago.* By this time, most of the overlying volcanic mountains have eroded away, revealing the underlying granitic rock. The Merced River has eroded deeply into its canyon. And because rivers do their erosive work in the bottoms of their channels, the river canyon is shaped like a **V** in cross section.

B. *About 2 million years ago.* Earth's climate enters a period of alternate cooling and warming that sends a series of glaciers into Yosemite Valley, the last of which leaves about 15,000 years ago. At least one glacier fills Yosemite Valley to the brim. Glaciers, hundreds to thousands of feet thick, fill canyons, and the work they do is distributed broadly over the canyon walls and floor, forming a valley with a broad **U** shape.

C. *About 22,000 years ago.* For the last time, a glacier enters Yosemite Valley, flowing just past Bridalveil Fall and maybe a bit farther. As it melts back, it leaves a pile of rock across the valley called a "terminal moraine"—the Bridalveil moraine. The glacier pauses as it recedes leaving a recessional moraine—the El Capitan moraine—damming the Merced River, which backs up into a marshy lake.

D. *About 15,000 years ago.* As that lake fills in, the flat surface of the valley floor comes into existence.

E. *Today.* Wetlands left by the last glacial advance have filled in. Low points are wet meadows, although human tinkering of the flow of water through the valley has dried them somewhat. Rockfalls and debris flows, now the dominant erosional forces in Yosemite, add material to the sides of the valley.

F. *About 5 million years from now.* What will Yosemite look like? No one really knows. What matters is that it will be very different from now. Yosemite is a work of art that will never be completed.

ICE AGES AND CLIMATE CHANGES

The rise and fall of glaciers is intimately linked to changes in Earth's climate. If precipitation remains the same and temperatures cool, glaciers grow larger. If temperatures warm, glaciers shrink or disappear altogether.

This has happened many times in the past 2 million years. The last glacier to enter Yosemite Valley reached its maximum about 20,000 years ago when it reached the far western end of the valley. This last glaciation, called the Tioga glaciation, is named after Tioga Pass, the high point along the Tioga Road. It had melted completely away by 10,000 years ago. These changes in climate will no doubt continue to occur in the future.

It appears that our planet is entering a new warming period, and the few small glaciers left in the Sierra will probably be gone long before the end of the twenty-first century. How long this warm period will last and how hot it will get we can't know for sure, but changes will no doubt take place in the composition of plant and animal communities in Yosemite. Will temperatures cool again? Will glaciers return to the valley? How will we humans respond to the changes?

THE BIOLOGICAL SETTING

While geologists may prefer to look at a barren landscape uncluttered with plants and animals, the rest of us generally feel more comfortable in the presence of living things. Yosemite National Park is a place with a broad diversity of life.

Variety Is the Spice of Life

Travel the world over, and you'll find about thirty-five locations where the number of plant and animal species is unusually high. These places are known as biodiversity hotspots, and California is one of them. One thing California shares in common with 20 percent of these important locations is a climate

Left: Dudleya. *Right top:* yellow velvet beetle on bistort flower. *Middle:* crab spider on California coneflower. *Bottom:* California sister.

typified by hot, dry summers and cool, wet winters—a Mediterranean climate.

In addition to climate type, California's mountains create stratified zones where varying temperature and precipitation create a variety of local climates. Because of these layered life zones, many climatic niches can be exploited by a larger variety of species.

Because of its climate type and geographic variety, Yosemite boasts more than 1,400 kinds of vascular plants: ferns and their relatives, cone-bearing trees, broad-leaved trees, shrubs, wildflowers, and other plants, including grasses and similar-looking species. Nearly 200 types of mosses and their allies find suitable habitat here.

In addition to the numerous plant communities and associations, there are uncounted spiders, bugs, beetles, moths, butterflies, and the like; 262 species of birds, 80 of mammals, 20 of reptiles, and 9 of amphibians that run, gallop, walk, soar, fly, flutter, hop, crawl, and slither throughout the park.

Some, like unicellular organisms, are so small we need microscopes to see them. Some, like bears, weigh hundreds of pounds. Some, like ground squirrels, Steller's jays, and ravens, are ever present while others, like moles, shrews, and salamanders, live out their cryptic lives in the soil, inside rotting logs, or otherwise hidden.

All of this variety provides the spice of life in Yosemite, and the diversity also provides for stability of life in the environment.

Tuolumne Meadows 8,600 ft.

White Wolf 7,800 ft.

Tenaya Lake

Crane Flat 6,192 ft.

Yosemite Valley 4,000 ft.

Upper Montane Zone 6,000–8,500 ft.

El Portal 2,000 ft.

Lower Montane Zone 3,500–6,000 ft.

Foothill Zone 500–3,500 ft.

Life Zones of Yosemite

Life Zones

Yosemite's mountains provide environments for plants and animals similar to what you might see on a trip from Mexico to northern Alaska. You can actually see this on a 2-hour drive from El Portal, at about 2,000 feet, to Tioga Pass, at nearly 10,000 feet, where nearby peaks rise 2,000 to 3,000 feet higher.

At the lowest elevations, the foothill zone is like the hot, dry lands of Mexico. As you move higher, forests become the dominant features of the montane zones, looking like the middle to northern latitudes of the United States and Canada. The mountains above tree line rise into the alpine zone—the mountain version of the tundra of northern Alaska above the Arctic Circle.

It's Complicated

Nothing in nature is as neat and clean as illustrations in a book. Many things contribute to variations in climate. For instance, the elevations of these zones tend to be lower on the cooler northern sides of mountains or in the bottoms of canyons, where cold air collects.

In addition, on east-facing slopes, the ground receives sunlight during the cooler part of the day, while western slopes get direct sun during warmer afternoons. Consequently, western slopes are dryer and support a flora more tolerant of dry conditions.

The life zones illustration below shows typified life zones and some of the main trees, shrubs, wildflowers, and wildlife common to each.

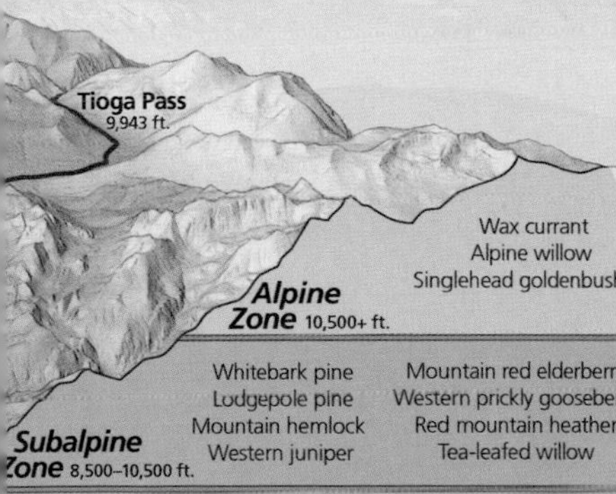

Tioga Pass
9,943 ft.

Alpine Zone 10,500+ ft.

Subalpine Zone 8,500–10,500 ft.

TREES	SHRUBS	WILDFLOWERS	WILDLIFE
	Wax currant Alpine willow Singlehead goldenbush	Alpine shooting star Alpine columbine Davidson penstemon Sky pilot Alpine daisy	Sierra Nevada bighorn sheep American pika Yellow-bellied marmot Sierra Nevada yellow-legged frog
Whitebark pine Lodgepole pine Mountain hemlock Western juniper	Mountain red elderberry Western prickly gooseberry Red mountain heather Tea-leafed willow	Subalpine shooting star Whorled penstemon Large-leaved lupine Dwarf lousewort	Yellow-bellied marmot Belding's ground squirrel Pine marten Long-tailed weasel Clark's nutcracker
Red fir Lodgepole pine Quaking aspen Jeffrey pine Western white pine Giant sequoia	Huckleberry oak Greenleaf manzanita Pinemat manzanita Mountain whitethorn Bush chinquapin	Jeffrey's shooting star Crimson columbine Scarlet gilia Pride of the mountains	American black bear Northern flying squirrel Chickaree Golden-mantled ground squirrel Sooty grouse Coyote
Giant sequoia White fir Incense-cedar Douglas-fir Ponderosa pine Black oak	Whiteleaf manzanita Deerbrush Bitter cherry	Jeffrey's shooting star Self-heal Meadow goldenrod White-veined shinleaf	American black bear California ground squirrel Pacific fisher Coyote Western gray squirrel Steller's jay
Gray pine Interior live oak Blue oak California buckeye	Whiteleaf manzanita Buckbrush Toyon Yerba santa Redbud	California saxifrage Henderson's shooting star Tufted poppy Popcorn flower Woolly Indian paintbrush	American black bear Bobcat Mountain lion Raccoon Striped skunk Scrub jay

WILDLIFE

There are certain animals you will probably see at some of the turnouts in Yosemite because they have learned to beg for food. Common beggars include ground squirrels, chipmunks, marmots, Steller's jays, ravens, deer, raccoons, coyotes, and bears.

Please don't feed them. It takes away some of their wildness, which national parks are supposed to protect. It's not only dangerous to humans to feed roadside animals, it also encourages them to linger by the road, making it more likely they'll be hit by cars.

All of the animals can bite, and some may carry diseases, so please just enjoy them from a distance.

Yosemite lacks the kind of habitat needed to support large herd animals like bison or elk, but mule deer are often seen in forests, meadows, and chaparral.

Squirrels are ubiquitous and come in many varieties. Look for California ground squirrels at lower elevations, golden-mantled ground squirrels at middle elevations, and Belding's ground squirrels at higher elevations. Gray squirrels, Douglas squirrels, and flying squirrels live in the trees,

Left to right: Top: yellow-bellied marmot, raven. *Middle:* American black bear, mule deer. *Bottom:* Belding's ground squirrel, bobcat.

and several chipmunk species reside at middle to high elevations.

Along with these animals are their predators. The main predator of deer is the mountain lion. These natives of the Americas are rarely seen. People report seeing bobcats now and again in Yosemite Valley, and while bobcats have been known to eat deer, they mostly hunt smaller animals like squirrels.

Coyotes are often seen mousing in the meadows or trotting through forests. Raccoons, like coyotes and bears, are opportunistic feeders. You may encounter them in campgrounds or at any of the lodging or food service areas in Yosemite Valley, Wawona, or El Portal, exploiting the opportunities these places provide.

If you see a bear, the wildlife office would like to hear about it. Call (209) 372-0322 and leave a message with details of your sighting: where, when, what the animal was doing, and tag color and number if you notice that.

THE HUMAN STORY

If space on the page were meted out based on the length of time various peoples were connected with Yosemite, this booklet would be mostly about American Indians. Only the last two or three pages would be about the modern development of Yosemite into a national park.

Some research suggests that groups of hunter-gatherers, wielding spears and atlatls (specialized tools for throwing projectiles accurately at great velocity) and carrying portable seed-grinding stones, may have wandered through the foothills and into the mountains in pursuit of game more than 10,000 years ago.

Who they were or what they called themselves can't even be guessed

We do know that various cultures speaking different languages passed through what we now call Yosemite for thousands of years. We also know that a major change took place in hunting technology and diet some 1,500 years ago, when atlatls were given up for the bow and arrow. It was also at about this time when people here began to use bedrock mortars and eat acorn as a primary staple.

This last period appears to be when the most recent culture lived at the lower elevations of the park, including Yosemite Valley, and west into the foothills. At this time, California had an incredibly diverse assemblage of cultures speaking many different languages—more than Europe has today.

For thousands of years, American Indians cared for Yosemite and called it home. Here they were born, and here they died. Here they were schooled in the ways of their parents and grandparents, and here they fell in love, married, raised families, and felt the fears, joys, and sorrows typical of all human beings. They cared for this valley for countless generations until they were forcibly removed in 1851. They were allowed to return, but the valley was no longer under their control.

The new managers of Yosemite Valley would not allow the Indians to burn the meadows and forests of the valley or the surrounding mountains as they had done for generations. Regularly set fires as well as naturally caused fires had kept the landscape open and the plants productive of food—especially acorn-bearing oaks—and basket-making materials.

The culture of the newcomers clashed with that of the people who depended upon the agricultural use of fire to keep the land open and parklike. Ironically, this openness is one of the features of Yosemite Valley that so appealed to early tourists and that is now mostly gone.

The first sightseeing parties began visiting Yosemite Valley in the summer of 1855. Among those first tourists was artist Thomas Ayres, who drew the first sketches of the valley. Almost immediately after its discovery by outsiders, Yosemite Valley began to inspire thought that was virtually unheard of in the history of land use: that this inspirational scenery should be protected from utilitarian use and that it should not be privately owned.

Above and right: Thomas Ayres sketched Yosemite Valley in 1855.

Within nine years, the U.S. Congress entrusted Yosemite Valley and the Mariposa Grove of Big Trees (known now as the Mariposa Grove of Giant Sequoias) to the state of California to protect essentially as a state park under the Yosemite Grant, which stated that "the premises shall be held for public use, resort, and recreation; and shall be inalienable for all time." President Abraham Lincoln signed the bill on June 30, 1864, creating the first such designated wild land in the United States.

Entrepreneurs built toll trails and primitive accommodations, and for the next ten years the only way to get to Yosemite Valley was by foot or horseback.

In the early 1870s, "civilization" would reach the valley in the form of the Cosmopolitan, a saloon and bathhouse. Here you could get a hot bath and relax with such cocktails as a mint julep, a corpse reviver, or a Samson with the hair on. The Cosmopolitan had pool tables, full-length mirrors, and baths. Amazingly, all the furnishings were packed in on the backs of mules along twenty miles of rugged trail without one item being damaged.

The outlying communities of Mariposa, Coulterville, and Big Oak Flat competed for post-mining tourist trade by supporting trail and road builders. Turnpike companies raced to be the first to open toll roads to Yosemite Valley.

Ultimately, the Coulterville Road was the first to open, when about fifty wagons and carriages rolled into the valley on June 18, 1874. There were fireworks and bonfires on the cliffs, a quarter-mile procession, and a great deal of celebration. Twenty-nine days later, the Big Oak Flat Road opened, and the following spring the Wawona Road opened for business.

In 1890, Yosemite National Park was created, but the Yosemite Grant continued as a state park until the state receded the land in 1905 and the federal government accepted it in 1906.

The first automobiles entered the park at the beginning of the twentieth century, but they were quickly banned. Still, progress could not be stopped. Cars were allowed in Yosemite in 1913, and two years later, motor stages replaced horse-drawn stages in the park. Beginning in 1907, the Yosemite Valley Railway conveyed passengers quickly and comfortably to El Portal, where they were carried a short distance to Yosemite Valley by stage.

With each successive improvement in transportation to the valley, visitation increased. Horse trails gave way to wagon roads, wagon roads to automobile roads, and seasonal roads to year-round highways.

In 1925, visitation to Yosemite Valley was 209,166. In the summer of 1926, the All-Year Highway (California State Highway 140) opened. The next year, visitation more than doubled (490,430), causing serious crowding problems, especially on holiday weekends that summer. Ever since then, Yosemite Valley has been plagued by issues brought on by ever-increasing numbers of nature lovers.

The National Park Service continually works toward managing visitors while protecting the scenic wonders, plants, animals, and artifacts for future generations. The year 2014 marks the 150th anniversary of protecting Yosemite Valley and the Mariposa Grove.

The Cosmopolitan saloon and bathhouse, circa 1870.

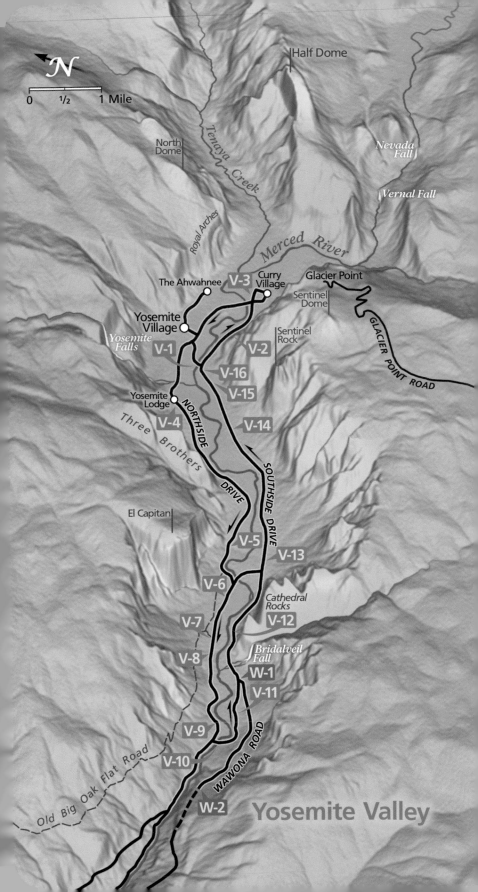

A Tour of Yosemite Valley

The tour of Yosemite Valley begins at the Sentinel Bridge parking area and proceeds east to Curry Village, loops back to the west end of Yosemite Valley, and returns to the starting point.

Yosemite Valley is indeed a very special place. It's only about 7 miles long. The valley floor averages about $3/4$ mile across and is very flat. The Merced River meanders through it, dropping less than 60 feet between the campgrounds in the eastern end of the Valley and the western end of El Capitan Meadow, a distance of about 6 miles. In cross section, cliffs plunge into the flat valley bottom at slightly less than vertical angles. The rim of Yosemite Valley rises approximately 3,000 feet, while the bottom is about 4,000 feet above sea level.

To begin the tour, find your way to the Sentinel Bridge parking area. It's marked **V-1** on the map on the facing page.

V-1 STONE TEMPLE

Famed nineteenth-century naturalist John Muir called Yosemite Valley the "sanctum sanctorum" ("holy of holies") of the Sierra Nevada:

It is by far the grandest of all of the special temples of Nature I was ever permitted to enter.

JOHN MUIR, LETTER TO
MRS. EZRA S. CARR, JULY 26, 1868

Take a moment to enjoy the views from the meadows here. Two paved paths lead from the parking area. Facing Yosemite Falls, one path is toward the right side of the parking area; the other is toward the left. Take the path on the left, and walk about 100 yards to get to the a broad view of the Valley.

These temple walls are made of what geologists call plutonic rock, named for Pluto, god of the underworld. All the rock you see from here originated deep within Earth. How deep? Geologists say 3 to 5 miles. If that's the case, how did these trillions and

View of Yosemite Falls by moonlight from across the Valley.

trillions of tons of granite get lifted to where they are today? And what source of energy could be so vast it could do that kind of lifting?

If it were possible to ride an oceanic plate as it subducted beneath a continental plate (see "Geologic Story," page 11), you would heat up to temperatures of thousands of degrees. At the same time, incredible pressures would build. This heat would melt rocks all around you. As rock heats and liquifies, it expands, becoming less dense, and rises (much as hot air in a balloon makes it rise through cooler air). This melted rock is called magma while it is underground.

Sometimes magma reaches the surface, forming volcanoes where it oozes, pours, or spews out of the ground. The melted rock that erupts from them is then called lava.

When magma remains in chambers inside Earth, it cools slowly over thousands of years. Various minerals in the magma begin to crystallize, and if cooling is slow enough, the crystals will become very large (about a quarter of an inch) and

tightly interlocked, ultimately making for very strong rock.

The physical grandeur of Yosemite Valley has to do with the age-old struggle between rising mountains and the erosive forces that wear them down, tempered by the structure of the rock. In this case, flowing water, primarily, cut a canyon about 3,000 feet deep where Yosemite Valley would be. The exact location of this canyon was determined by weaknesses in the rock.

Rock Is Weak?

Yosemite is made up primarily of granitic rock that solidified miles below a volcanic mountain range about 100 million to 80 million years ago. The character of Yosemite's scenery follows cracks in the rock that control the angular shapes of the mountains and canyon walls.

Granite characteristically breaks along planes. Some of those breaks, which geologists call "joints," extend from about Half Dome to the Yosemite Falls area of the valley, then from just west of there to the Three Brothers, then again from there past

El Capitan, giving Yosemite Valley its overall zigzag shape. When viewed from the air, the landscape of Yosemite is crisscrossed with lines of vegetation showing where master joints traverse the landscape. The granitic rock of Yosemite Valley is somewhat unusual in that much of it is massive and broken with relatively few joints, although some granites in the Valley are more jointed.

Look at the cliffs across the Valley in the neighborhood of Yosemite Falls. The cliffs there are made up of El Capitan Granite, a very strong and relatively unfractured rock. Now

Aerial view of Yosemite covering about 2 square miles. Vegetation reveals lines of weakness called "joints."

scan to the right. There is a canyon that isn't so vertical. That's Indian Canyon. The rock there is Sentinel Granodiorite, which tends to fracture more readily and causes a break in the cliffs. Scanning farther to the right, the sheer cliffs return with a newer, stronger type of granite called Half Dome Granodiorite.

Michelangelo believed that each block of stone had a figure hidden inside and that it was the sculptor's task to free it. And so it is with the cliffs and stone monuments of Yosemite Valley. For tools, the master sculptor uses the force of gravity, water, and ice.

When you are ready, turn right out of the parking area, then left at the stop sign.

V-1 to **V-2** is 0.7 mile. **V-2** will be on your right.

V-2 LECONTE MEMORIAL LODGE

Midsummer 1870, Joseph LeConte, a professor at the University of California at Berkeley and a founding member of the Sierra Club, took a trip to Yosemite with a group of his students. On the morning of August 5, he met a young man working at a sawmill near the base of Yosemite Falls. This man turned out to be John Muir. At the time, Muir was not as well known as he later would become, but he and LeConte had a mutual friend who had advised them both to get in touch with each other.

Two days later, Muir joined LeConte's party for a seven-day journey across the Sierra. Muir was excited to find a receptive ear for his theories about how the mountain landscapes were glacially formed, and LeConte became the first scientist to sup-

Plaque honoring Joseph LeConte at the LeConte Memorial Lodge.

port John Muir's belief that much of Yosemite was shaped by glaciers. However, he believed the extent of glacial work was much less than what Muir thought.

John Muir would eventually become the first Sierra Club president and Joseph LeConte one of its charter members. In 1901, club members gathered at Camp Curry (now Curry Village) in preparation for the first Sierra Club wilderness outing. LeConte died at that gathering in Camp Curry. He was seventy-six.

Joseph LeConte was a dearly loved professor of geology and a highly regarded scientist. In his memory, the Sierra Club, in cooperation with the State Board of Yosemite Commissioners (Yosemite Valley was still a state park at the time), built the LeConte Memorial Lodge about a mile east at Camp Curry (now Curry Village), replacing a cottage that the club had been operating for a few years as a visitor center for the Yosemite Grant. The building was moved in 1919 to its current location at the base of the pile of rocks fallen from the near-vertical cliffs above.

John White, a Berkeley architect, designed the lodge, with the belief that the structure should be derived from native materials and built to capture the essence, scale, and color

of Yosemite Valley. It was dedicated on July 3, 1904, and continues to be operated by the Sierra Club under a cooperative agreement with the National Park Service. The LeConte Memorial Lodge has also been designated a national historic landmark for its significance in the area of conservation, as the principal foothold of the Sierra Club in the mountains from which they took their name.

Curry Village

Along the way to the next stop, you'll pass through the parking area for Curry Village. Here you may find cabins and tent cabins for accommodations, as well as a small market/gift shop, cafeteria, pizzeria, and a mountaineering shop.

Camp Curry began in 1899 when two schoolteachers decided to provide accommodations that were less expensive than the hotels but offered more services than the campgrounds. This was camp living at its best: Twelve dollars a week would get you a tent, a good table, and a clean napkin at every meal—and no tipping!

Continue along the one-way road to the next stop sign, and then turn right. Then turn left at the next road, and left again at the next intersection. The large meadow on your right will be Stoneman Meadow. Stop there.

V-2 to **V-3** is 0.7 mile. **V-3** will be on your right.

V-3 STONEMAN MEADOW

The American Indians of Yosemite Valley shared a few traditional stories with non-natives in the mid- to late 1800s. One story tells of a woman named Tissiack and her husband. They were walking through Yosemite Valley one hot day from some distant place. Both were irritated and quarrelsome. Eventually Tissiack

LeConte Memorial Lodge.

Royal Arches, North Dome, Washington Column, and Half Dome as seen from Stoneman Meadow.

stomped off ahead of her husband until she reached Mirror Lake. Hot and thirsty, she drank deeply from the cool waters, and by the time her husband arrived, the lake was dry. Enraged, he scolded her. She yelled back and they bickered. He hit her with his stick and she threw her burden basket at him.

A powerful spirit saw this terrible behavior and decided to put a stop to it. He turned Tissiack and her husband into stone mountains facing each other for eternity. She became Half Dome and he North Dome. The Indian name for Half Dome is Tissiack, and if you have a good imagination, you can make out her face stained with tears.

Look to the left at the round dome across from her. That's her husband, North Dome. Behind him is Basket Dome, the basket she threw at him. Below North Dome on the cliff, there are some expansive arches called the Royal Arches. They are the visor part of the cradle basket she was carrying.

On your way to the next stop, you will pass Yosemite Village, Yosemite Falls, and Yosemite Lodge.

Yosemite Village

Yosemite Village consists of the park's administrative headquarters, the Yosemite Museum, the Yosemite Cemetery (see page 40), the Valley Visitor Center, the Ansel Adams Gallery, the Wilderness Center, the Post Office, Degnan's Deli and Loft, the Village Store, the Village Grill, the Sport Shop, and the Art and Education Center. Information about these shops can be found in the park newspaper, the *Yosemite Guide*.

Yosemite Falls

Once past Yosemite Village, you will come to an open meadow on the left. At the far end of that meadow, you may find parking along the side of the road. The Yosemite Valley tour began on the opposite side of the meadow from there.

Many people take the shuttle bus here to enjoy a short walk to Lower Yosemite Fall. The total drop of the upper and lower falls together is 2,425 feet. The stroll around the loop trail is pleasant, but be aware that Yosemite Falls usually diminish considerably by mid- to late July, earlier in a dry year.

Yosemite Lodge

Yosemite Lodge will be on your left after you pass Yosemite Falls. This property stands on the former site of the U.S. Cavalry post. The cavalry administered Yosemite National Park before the National Park Service was created by Congress in 1916. Some of the old cavalry buildings were still in use in the 1950s.

To continue with the tour, drive to the next intersection, turn right, and drive 2 miles. The next stop will be on the right after you pass Yosemite Falls and Yosemite Lodge.

V-3 to **V-4** is 2.0 miles. **V-4** will be on your right.

V-4 CAMP 4

There is indeed something very special about the rock in Yosemite Valley. That's why so many rock climbers descend on this campground when the weather is good—usually from May through October. Camp 4 is a sort of United Nations of climbers.

On a walk through Camp 4, you will hear many languages spoken: English, Spanish, French, Chinese, Japanese, Korean, and Russian, to name a few.

Over the years, this campground has been the world's center of innovation for climbing techniques and technology. Because of this and the fact that it played a significant role in the development of rock climbing as a sport, Camp 4 was listed on the National Register of Historic Places in 2003.

The trail to the top of Yosemite Falls begins here. This confuses many hikers because this trail is not in the same place as the trail to Lower Yosemite Fall. Trails are confined to locations where they can be built. Trail builders have a practical knowledge of the structure of rock in Yosemite Valley. Utilizing this knowledge, John Conway built the trail to the top of Yosemite Falls in the 1870s, up a tree-covered talus slope to a series of ledges that led around to the foot of the upper fall. From there the trail zigzags up a steep ravine to the top of the cliffs.

The Middle Brother talus pile after 1920s rockfall. A major rockfall in 1987 added another 1.8 million tons of granite to it.

Cathedral Rocks

Cathedral Spires

Above: Wosky Pond with the Cathedral Spires and the Cathedral Rocks in the background.

Left: Tree frog.

Middle Brother Rockfall

Ahead, after you pass Camp 4, you may see a sign advising you not to stop. This is because of the danger of falling rocks in one of the most active rockfall areas in the park. Periodically, rocks fall from the cliffs above and sometimes hit the road. As you drive past, glance at the huge pile of boulders that have fallen.

On March 10, 1987, a tremendous piece of the middle prominence of the Three Brothers broke loose, disintegrated, and fell 2,600 feet down the cliff. An estimated 1.8 million tons of granite came down in that event, making it the largest in the recorded history of Yosemite. Think of all that rock adding to the talus pile on your right as you pass. Unbelievably, that pile of talus is so large that before and after photographs don't look all that different.

V-4 to V-5 is 1.9 miles. V-5 will be on your left.

V-5 WOSKY POND

Note the depression in the foreground. In the winter, spring, and early summer, it fills with water. Wosky Pond, as it is called locally, is named for John B. Wosky, a resident landscape architect for the National Park Service in Yosemite from 1928 to 1933 and assistant superintendent from 1935 to 1952, who got his car stuck in the mud here.

People often see mallard ducklings swimming about the pond with their mom. In the evenings, beginning sometime in February, you can hear a chorus of tree frogs singing their hearts out (sometimes even when it's snowing).

The meadow stretching from here out into the trees is known locally as Slaughterhouse Meadow. In the early days, it was impractical to get fresh meat delivered this far out in the mountains. Beef raised on Yosemite's meadows was killed and cut into meat at a slaughterhouse here.

Between here and the next stop, you'll see that the Merced River flows

El Capitan's North America Wall. Note the 80-foot ponderosa pine in the overhang.

straight toward the road and then makes a 180-degree bend, known locally as Devils Elbow—more about that bend at the next stop.

V-5 to **V-6** is 0.3 mile. **V-6** will be on your right.

V-6 EL CAPITAN

A spectacular view of the massive eastern face of El Capitan presents itself just a few easy steps from the marker post toward the cliff. Look for the clearing in the trees to the right of the V-6 post. From there you will see the face towering nearly 3,000 feet above.

The photograph shows where to look for an 80-foot ponderosa pine tree growing in an alcove on the sheer face of El Capitan. That tree is more than 300 years old and is growing in cracks in the rocks that form a series of shelves supporting quite a few plants. Wildflowers grow up there in the spring, their colorful faces unseen by the throngs of people below.

When you are ready to continue with the tour, take notice of the hill that extends along the right side of the road. The following story is fictional but reflects a possible occurrence related to that hill.

Yosemite Valley 3,600 Years Ago

The river flows past a small village near Tu-toc-a-nu-la, "the Rock Chief" (today we call it "El Capitan"). Conical bark-covered houses called "oo-ma-chas" stand here and there. It's a cold evening in spring, and the entire village is asleep. A great horned owl hoots nearby.

Suddenly the ground begins to shake. The earthquake wakes everyone in the village just in time to hear a loud and terrible noise sounding from the top of Tu-toc-a-nu-la. It's so loud! Rushing from their oo-ma-chas, some see an avalanche of fire as granite chunks spark against one another in the dark.

Eight million tons of rock crash to the ground and rumble across the landscape. In seconds, the entire village is buried under twenty feet of stone, and a dense cloud of fine granite dust rolls up the opposite canyon wall.

The next morning dawns over a drastically changed scene. The Merced River no longer flows west through meadowlands as it did the previous day. Instead, a huge pile of fresh white boulders extending far into the valley has turned the river sharply to the south and across the valley.

The scene is not a colorful one. Everything is a shade of gray—gray pines, gray oaks, gray meadows. Dust from the previous night's rock avalanche has settled on everything. In some places, it's several inches thick. Overnight an immense change has taken place—just as it has so many times since the last glacier left the valley 15,000 years ago.

We don't really know if there was a village beneath that event, but we do know that people lived in Yosemite Valley at the time. We also know the rocks fell all at once, and we know it happened about 3,600 years ago. We know there was a huge earthquake centered on the east side of the Sierra Nevada at about the same time as the rock avalanche.

We know the event changed the course of the river. The evidence is here. Look for the rock pile that extends from nearby and along the road. Notice, too, how the river makes an abrupt turn and parallels the rocks. This is but one incident in a long history of powerful events that have continued to shape Yosemite since the glaciers last scraped along the bases of these cliffs.

V-6 to V-7 is 0.9 mile. **V-7** will be on your right.

V-7 EL CAPITAN MORAINE / OLD BIG OAK FLAT ROAD

The Old Big Oak Flat Road wound down through the trees to your right, and continued on into the valley.

Here is a great place to get out and stretch your legs. A 20-minute round-trip walk will bring you into intimate contact with a piece of the geologic puzzle of how Yosemite Valley came to look the way it does. Across the road, there is a hill—not a round hill,

The El Capitan recessional moraine is easily seen when snow is on the ground

but a long hill. This hill, or ridge, goes all the way across the valley from here. There is no trail, but it's fairly easy to walk along the top of the ridge until you get to the river. Return to your car by reversing direction.

The hill is a glacial moraine—a pile of rocks, gravel, sand, and silt that was deposited by a glacier. In this case, about 19,000 years ago, a retreating glacier paused here long enough to dump mountain debris at its end, or terminus. (See "Geologic Story," page 11.)

You can investigate for yourself. As you walk along the moraine, look closely at the rocks that sit on top of it. See if you can find some that have rather large rectangular crystals in them. These crystals often stand out as squared-off knobs.

When you find one, consider this. No bedrock anywhere near here looks like it. The nearest rocks of this type are from beyond Yosemite Valley, many miles up valley. This type of rock is called Cathedral Peak Granodiorite, and it was carried here from at least 15 miles up canyon.

Cathedral Peak Granodiorite. Note the large rectangular feldspar crystals.

V-7 to **V-8** is 0.3 mile. **V-8** will be on your left.

V-8 BRIDALVEIL FALL

Look up the definition of "hanging valley," and there's a good chance you'll find a picture of Bridalveil Fall. When a side stream joins a larger stream, they typically meet at the same elevation. Such was probably the case when Bridalveil Creek joined the Merced River long before the ice ages (see "Geologic Story," page 11), although there may have been a series of cascades along the creek as it flowed into the Merced River.

Bridalveil Fall tumbles from its hanging valley.

The landscape scene from Valley View.

Then came the mighty glaciers of the ice ages. The glaciers that flowed down through Yosemite Valley were larger and more powerful than the few smaller glaciers that excavated Bridalveil Valley. The difference in erosive power left Bridalveil Valley hanging 620 feet up the cliff.

V-8 to **V-9** is 0.8 mile. **V-9** will be on your left.

V-9 VALLEY VIEW

In 1916, a fourteen-year-old boy caught his first glimpse of Yosemite from here. His family had been thinking about a vacation to Santa Cruz or Puget Sound, but he had other ideas. A month or so earlier, he had been given a book to read while he was convalescing with a cold. The book, *In the Heart of the Sierras*, by James Mason Hutchings, was filled with fantastic descriptions of Yosemite Valley.

The boy was so taken by the book that he began a campaign to vacation in Yosemite. His parents eventually agreed, and on June 1, they boarded the 6:00 a.m. train to Yosemite. It took all day to get to El Portal, where they spent the night.

The next morning, his family headed for Yosemite Valley in an open tour bus. When they arrived here at Valley View, the scene opened before the boy. Half a century later, he recalled that "the splendor of Yosemite burst upon us and it *was* glorious. Little clouds were gathering in the sky above the granite cliffs, and the mists of Bridal Veil shimmered in the sun."

Later on that trip, his parents gave the boy a Kodak No. 1 Box Brownie camera. Each time he pressed the shutter, light bounced off the river, the trees, the wildflowers, the waterfalls, and the great cliffs and streamed through the cheap lens of his camera. Trillions of photons showered onto the film that would magically store the images of what his camera had seen. This was to be the first roll of film taken of Yosemite by the world-famous nature photographer Ansel Adams.

Since then, millions of amateur and professional photographers alike have captured this scene, and it hasn't worn out yet. So go ahead, take out your camera, and shoot away. Maybe you won't become the next famous nature photographer, but you can experience the magic of capturing your own memories of Yosemite.

You may see two waterfalls from Valley View. Bridalveil Fall, the most easily seen, spills over the cliff straight across the valley, whereas Ribbon Fall tumbles to the far left of the scene. Bridalveil Fall drops 620 feet year round. Ribbon Fall, on the other hand, dries up in early summer, but it is the tallest single drop of all Yosemite's waterfalls—a whopping 1,612 feet. That's nearly a third of a mile!

You may have noticed the sign on the south edge of the parking area indicating the high-water mark for the flood of January 2, 1997. Had you been standing here at that time, you wouldn't have been standing at all. You would have been swimming for your life—more about that at the next stop.

To continue on the Yosemite Valley tour, get in the left lane and turn left at the stop sign. Stop immediately after you cross Pohono Bridge.

If you are headed for Highway 120 (east to Highway 395 or west toward Manteca and San Francisco) or Highway 140 (toward Mariposa and Merced), keep to the right and stop at the parking area on your right 1 mile from here. There you can read the introduction to the road you intend to drive. The Big Oak Flat Road goes to Highway 120, and the El Portal Road connects with Highway 140.

If you are continuing on the Valley tour or are headed for Highway 41 (south toward Fresno), keep to the left, cross the bridge, and stop at V-10.

V-9 to V-10 is 0.2 mile. V-10 will be on your left.

V-10 POHONO BRIDGE

The bridge you just crossed is called Pohono Bridge, after the American Indian name for Bridalveil Fall (see **W-1** on page 24). You may have noticed a structure just upstream. That is the Pohono Bridge streamgaging station. It measures the flow of the Merced River and was underwater during the peak flow of the January 2, 1997 flood. The estimated river flow past here was approximately 25,000 cubic feet per second. That's 1.5 million pounds of water blasting past every second! Imagine the power that much water carries with it. The torrent was so powerful that it pushed

Large Tree Specimens

Two great examples of tree species not common in Yosemite Valley grow on either side of the road here. On the upstream side of the road stands a huge Douglas-fir, and a sugar pine grows on the downstream side. Both trees can be readily identified by their cones. The sugar pine has the longest cones in the world. They frequently measure 18 to 20 inches long and can reach lengths over 2 feet. The Douglas-fir cones are much smaller and can be identified by the three-pointed bracts sticking out from underneath the cone scales (see picture below).

Douglas-fir and sugar pine cones (not to scale).

huge boulders downstream like marbles in the stream of a fire hose. Floodwaters ripped up a six-inch-thick slab of pavement on the bridge a full lane in diameter and rotated it 90 degrees.

V-10 to V-11 is 0.4 mile. V-11 will be on your right.

V-11 HISTORIC ENCAMPMENTS

The historic marker here commemorates the meeting of Sierra Club president John Muir and President Theodore Roosevelt. They camped near here in 1903 and talked "forest good."

Fifty-two years earlier, another historic encampment occurred near here. Hostilities between the Indians of Yosemite Valley and miners in the foothills led to the creation of the Mariposa Battalion—a state militia composed of civilian volunteers—to rein in the natives of the Yosemite region. The ensuing Mariposa War led to the discovery of the Valley by non-Indians in 1851. On that first night in Yosemite Valley, members of the Mariposa Battalion camped near here. Yellow flames of the campfire warmed the faces of the men as they sat surrounded by the gathering darkness with El Capitan looming nearby.

Lafayette Bunnell, a private in that group, suggested naming the valley:

Different names were proposed, but none were satisfactory to a majority of our circle. Some romantic and foreign names were offered, but I observed that a very large number were canonical and Scripture names. From this I inferred that I was not the only one in whom religious emotions or thoughts had been aroused by the mysterious power of the surrounding scenery.

At the same time, Bunnell also suggested that they:

… give the valley the name of Yo-sem-i-ty, as it was suggestive, euphonious, and certainly American; that by so doing, the name of the tribe of Indians which we met leaving their homes in this valley, perhaps never to return, would be perpetuated.

LAFAYETTE BUNNELL, *DISCOVERY OF THE YOSEMITE*, 1892

Interestingly, this was not the name given the valley locally. The Indian people called the valley Ahwahnee ("place like a gaping mouth"), and they called themselves Ahwahn eechee ("dwellers of Ahwahnee"). By naming the valley "Yo-sem-i-ty," the Mariposa Battalion actually named it "Killers" in the language of the Southern Sierra Miwok. This is presumably because the Indians in Yosemite were an assemblage of people from various tribes who may have been enemies to the Indians of the foothills.

Just thirteen years later, through the Yosemite Grant, Yosemite Valley became in essence a state park, and then, in 1890, the land surrounding this valley became a national park. John Muir eventually came to the conclusion that Yosemite Valley should be included in the national park, and when Theodore Roosevelt camped out with him, Muir convinced him that the Yosemite Grant should be placed under the federal protection of Yosemite National Park. Within a few years, it was done.

Side Trip to Tunnel View

There is a breathtaking overview of Yosemite Valley 1.5 miles up the Wawona Road and a very special view of Bridalveil Fall on your way back down to the Valley.

To make a short side trip to these views, stay in the right lane, make a right turn in .4 mile, and drive 1.5 miles up the Wawona Road to the large parking area on your right at Tunnel View. Here, while you enjoy the view, read some historical background for Tunnel View at **W-2** on page 88.

Return to the Valley the way you came, on the Wawona Road, and for a spectacular yet intimate view of Bridalveil Fall, take the next turn on the right (1.5 miles from Tunnel View) into the parking area. Then follow the short trail (0.5-mile round trip) to the viewing area. The trail is paved and becomes steep at the end but it's fairly short and worth the effort. In May or June, you may want to bring something to protect yourself from the mist.

Back in your car, turn right out of the parking area, continue onto the one-way road, and drive 1.3 miles to **V-12** on the Yosemite Valley tour.

V-11 to **V-12** is 1.7 miles (without the side trip to Tunnel View). **V-12** will be on your left.

V-12 CATHEDRAL SPIRES

The most active geologic force shaping Yosemite today is rockfall. We know that the Cathedral Spires were not formed by glaciers, for glaciers would have scraped away delicate spires like these. Instead these spires were formed by rockfall during the nearly 1 million years since the last huge glacier filled the Valley that high. Since that time the rock that once connected the spires has fallen away leaving them standing tall. Local Indian people called them Pu-si´-na Chuck´-ah, meaning "the mouse and the acorn granary."

V-12 to **V-13** is 0.4 mile. **V-13** will be on your right.

Cathedral Spires.

V-13 THREE BROTHERS

Yosemite scenery is, in fact, what it's cracked up to be. Major crack systems, or joints, provide weak areas where erosive forces may work to reveal shapes in the landscape.

The intersection of joints in three planes—two of them vertical and one diagonal—define the shape of the Three Brothers. The shaping continues as rock falls regularly, especially from the Middle Brother. The largest rockfall in Yosemite Valley since the 1850s fell from there in 1987. It's one of the most active rockfall areas in the park.

The Three Brothers were named for the three sons of Chief Tenaya, who were captured and taken prisoner

Three Brothers.

by the Mariposa Battalion. One was shot and killed trying to escape.

V-13 to **V-14** is 1.5 miles. **V-15** will be on your right.

V-14 SENTINEL ROCK / FOUR MILE TRAIL / LOWER VILLAGE

The stone feature towering more than 3,000 feet overhead is called Sentinel Rock for its imagined likeness to a gigantic watchtower. The area here in the shadow of Sentinel Rock was called the Lower Village. Two hotels, residences, a chapel, a photography studio, an art studio, stables, and the residence of Galen Clark, the first guardian of the Yosemite Grant, stood here in 1886. Near here also stood the tollhouse for the Four Mile Trail to Glacier Point. By 1901, most of these had fallen into disuse and the chapel was moved to the Upper Village, where it remains today. Today, all the buildings are gone, and tolls are no longer charged for the Four Mile Trail (see **G-7** on page 98).

V-14 to **V-15** is 0.4 mile. **V-15** will be on your left.

V-15 YOSEMITE FALLS VIEW

Along these meadows you will find excellent views of Yosemite Falls. The meadows are closed because of overuse. There is, however, a boardwalk that provides access to the area without damaging the meadow habitat. Unlike Bridalveil Fall (see **G-9** on page 98), which flows year round, Yosemite Falls usually dry up by late in the summer season (see **T-10** on page 62).

Sentinel Rock.

V-15 to **V-16** is 0.3 mile. **V-16** will be on your right.

V-16 OLD YOSEMITE VILLAGE

Here you are in a ghost town, where the once-bustling Upper Yosemite Village stood. The only building left is the Yosemite Chapel. It was built in 1879 in the Lower Village near the Four Mile Trail and later moved here. It is the oldest building still in use in Yosemite.

Some of the trees, including a sugar maple from the East Coast and several giant sequoias, still stand, and although the buildings are gone, the sidewalk across the street remains. The buildings either succumbed to fire or were razed as the new Yosemite Village, on the sunnier, warmer side of the valley, grew.

Look at the map of all the building sites on page 40 and wander about. Consider how active the area was, and how the National Park Service has returned it to a more natural state. Yes, the buildings are gone, but to those with imagination it is still a ghost town.

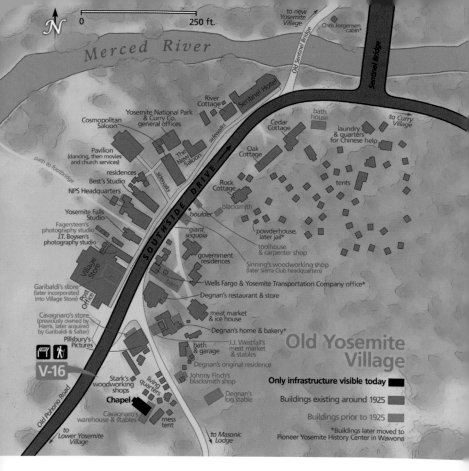

The Great Earthquake

On March 26, 1872, John Muir witnessed a large rockfall that fell near here:

I was aroused by an earthquake; and though I had never before enjoyed a storm of this sort, the strange, wild thrilling motion and rumbling could not be mistaken, and I ran out of my cabin, . . . shouting, "A noble earthquake!" . . . It was a calm moonlight night, and no sound was heard for the first minute or two save a low muffled underground rumbling and a slight rustling of the agitated trees, as if, in wrestling with the mountains, Nature were holding her breath. Then, suddenly, out of the strange silence and strange motion there came a tremendous roar. The Eagle Rock, a short distance up the valley, had given way, and I saw it falling in thousands of the great boulders I had been studying so long, pouring to the valley floor in a free curve luminous from friction, making a terribly sublime and beautiful spectacle—an arc of fire fifteen hundred feet span, as true in form and as steady as a rainbow, in the midst of the stupendous roaring rock-storm. . . . Storms of every sort, torrents, earthquakes, cataclysms, "convulsions of nature," etc., however mysterious and lawless at first sight they may seem, are only harmonious notes in the song of creation, varied expressions of God's love.

JOHN MUIR, *OUR NATIONAL PARKS*, 1901

When you are ready to leave, continue on the one-way road, make a left turn at the stop sign, and cross Sentinel Bridge. Pull into the parking area on the left, where you began the tour, and read the conclusion of the Yosemite Valley road tour below.

V-16 to **V-1** is 0.2 mile. **V-1** will be on your left.

V-1 END YOSEMITE VALLEY TOUR

If you've followed the Yosemite Valley tour and read the stories in this section, you know that everything about the Valley constantly changes—and these changes aren't always gentle. Rangers and other residents will tell you that they see changes every day and every season.

Old-timers will tell you they have seen massive rockslides, floods that have changed the course of the river, and fires that have changed forests to chaparral. Geologists will tell you dinosaurs once roamed a volcanic landscape that was here long before the granite of the Sierra Nevada was discovered by people thousands of years ago.

People have also had a profound effect on the landscape of Yosemite Valley. By harvesting the specific plants and animals they required for nutritional and cultural purposes, early American Indians changed biologic communities.

Fire, in particular, made for an open landscape, which the Ahwahneechee appreciated. They used this agricultural tool liberally. As a result, gold rush–era invaders, early tourists, and homesteaders enjoyed a wide, open valley with oak woodlands, a few conifers, and unobstructed views of towering monuments of stone and water.

Within nine years of the first tourists, Yosemite Valley had so inspired people that they were impelled to create a park, preserved for rest, resort, and contemplation of scenery so sublime as to generate feelings of religiousness and spirituality. That preservation idea spread from here to Yellowstone, and on to wild parks throughout the world.

John Muir called the Sierra Nevada a "gentle wilderness," and yet the peaceful beauty we see here is the result of powerful and seemingly violent acts of nature. But it doesn't take a rock avalanche to affect the sensibilities of people. It could be a particular flower or butterfly in a meadow—or perhaps the way the light falls on a granite cliff.

Has Yosemite touched you? Are you not changed even slightly? Consider what you might do to return the favor.

Climb the mountains and get their good tidings, Nature's peace will flow into you as sunshine flows into trees. The winds will blow their own freshness into you and the storms their energy, while cares will drop off like autumn leaves.

JOHN MUIR, *OUR NATIONAL PARKS*, 1909

Cathedral Rocks as seen from across El Capitan Meadow.

El Portal Road

0   1   2 Miles

El Portal Road

4.5

There is a parking area at the intersection of the El Portal Road and the Big Oak Flat Road where you may stop and read the introduction to this road tour.

The Coulterville toll road entered the Merced River canyon a few miles downstream from this intersection (see **E-2** on facing page). From there it snaked up the canyon and on into Yosemite Valley. The first carriages and wagons to be driven into Yosemite Valley rolled past this point in June of 1874. The day the Coulterville Road opened, fifty carriages streamed into Yosemite Valley with much fanfare and celebration. Thus began a new era of transportation in Yosemite. Before that, only people on foot or horseback could get into the Valley.

In 1907, the Yosemite Valley Railroad began carrying passengers from Merced, in California's Central Valley, to El Portal, about 7 miles west of Yosemite Valley. The National Park Service would not allow the railroad to build tracks all the way into the park, so to ferry people from the end

of the line in El Portal to Yosemite Valley, the company constructed a wagon road, known as the El Portal Road, to intersect with the Coulterville Road. By this time, tolls were no longer allowed to be charged inside the park, so the last segment of the Coulterville Road was free to the railroad company.

By 1912, most Yosemite visitors arrived via train and then wagon along this route, taking business away from the Coulterville Road as well as the two other toll roads into Yosemite Valley, ultimately leading to their bankruptcy.

When automobiles were permitted to enter Yosemite National Park in 1913, many were brought to El Portal on the Yosemite Valley Railroad and then driven up the wagon road. A new road opened in 1926 that wound its way up the Merced Canyon across the river from the railroad. Ironically, the new automobile road (the All-Year Highway, now known as State Route 140), which used the wagon road built by the Yosemite Valley

A Yosemite-bound train steams its way up Merced Canyon from Merced.

Railroad, caused a decline in train travel to Yosemite.

From the intersection of El Portal Road and Big Oak Flat Road to E-1 is 1.7 miles. E-1 will be on your right.

E-1 THE CASCADES

Above the road here is a beautiful waterfall that many people miss in their rush to and from Yosemite Valley.

A parking area across the street provides a starting point for a quiet picnic or a leisurely walk to the river, where you may see such birds as black phoebes, belted kingfishers, and American dippers. During winter storms, deer from Yosemite Valley often wander down here, where it snows less frequently and they can more easily find food.

E-1 to E-2 is 0.3 mile. E-2 will be on your right.

E-2 THE COULTERVILLE AND YO SEMITE TURNPIKE

The Coulterville Road is buried under the boulders in front of you. It began in the gold rush town of Coulterville and wound its way up to Crane Flat (the current junction of the Tioga Road and the Big Oak Flat Road). By 1872, a man named Dr. John Taylor McLean had bought up nearly all the Coulterville and Yo Semite Turnpike Company stock. Having petitioned the State Board of Yosemite Commissioners for the exclusive right to build a road into Yosemite Valley, he was confident he could recoup his expenses after completing the turnpike.

McLean rediscovered a grove of giant sequoias, naming it the Merced Grove because of its proximity to the Merced River. (This grove of giant sequoias had probably been seen by the Walker Party in 1833 [see page 65], and a man named Roney [no relation to the author] had also come across it in his travels.) Realizing the sequoia grove could become a selling point for his turnpike, McLean abandoned six miles of already constructed road to Crane Flat and changed the route farther to the south, through the small grove of giant sequoias. The Coulterville and Yo Semite Turnpike was completed on June 18, 1874, becoming the first wagon road into Yosemite Valley. The road descended precariously along the cliffs on the north side of the Merced Canyon until it reached the bottom where marker post E-2 currently stands. From there the road wound its way up the Merced Canyon and connected with a road on the north side of the Merced River, opening a new era of wheeled vehicles entering Yosemite Valley.

Meanwhile, the builders of the Big Oak Flat Road had been denied permission to complete their toll road, so they went over the heads of the State Board of Yosemite Com-missioners by going to the state legislature. In this way, they acquired permission to complete their road. McLean collected exclusive tolls on the Coulterville Road for only one month before the Big Oak Flat Road opened.

Years later, Dr. McLean, who had spent $71,000 to build the Coulterville Road and collected only $33,923.71 in tolls, tried to sell the road to the federal government. The government took no action, and McLean's family said he died a broken man three years later.

The Big Oak Flat Road became the preferred route to Yosemite Valley and fewer people used the Coulterville Road over the years. Buried by a rockslide in 1982, the Coulterville Road is now closed to cars. If you can make your way past the rockslide, the road beyond is open to hikers. Locally, this rockslide is known as the Cookie Crumble because this is

The opening of the All-Year Highway (State Route 140) in 1926. *Foreground, left to right:* California governor Friend Richardson; National Park Service director Stephen Mather; California State Highway Commission chairman Harvey Toy.

a rock climbing area named after a large slab that rock climbers refer to as the Cookie.

The Night the Cookie Crumbled

It was a dark and stormy night on April 3, 1982. Yes it really was! In fact, it had been a very wet winter and the ground was saturated with rainwater. At 10:05 on that evening, Ranger Dick Ewart left Yosemite Valley and headed toward El Portal. When he arrived at this point, a log and a large boulder the size of a VW Bug blocked his way. This happens now and again, so he calmly drove back to a nearby residence and used the phone to report the situation. "I think they'll need a front-end loader to clear the road," he said, thinking the job would take about an hour.

Dick went back to the log and boulder and decided to look around to see if any other debris had fallen. As he walked around the corner, the menacing face of a three-story-high rock loomed out of the darkness. Can you imagine what must have gone through his head? "I think they're gonna need a bigger truck" comes to mind.

The smell of freshly broken rock permeated the air as a steady rain continued to fall through the darkness. Excited and eager to learn the extent of the rockslide, Dick began to explore. At one point, he looked curiously at a small stream coming off the hillside and thought, *I don't remember a stream flowing here before.* There hadn't been. It was run-off from the broken sewer line buried beneath the road.

Every now and then he heard the sound of smaller rocks falling and boulders settling into position. He was now on the other side of the rockslide and below the road. Above him, lights from a car shone in the darkness from the far side of the slide. Dick clambered up the bank to the road.

Now imagine the perspective of the driver of the car parked in front of a different three-story boulder. It's rainy. It's misty. It's foggy. The headlights illuminate just a small area surrounded by the night and the storm when, out of the darkness, the visage of a soaking wet ranger climbs up the side of the road and approaches.

In 1927, the year after the All-Year Highway was opened, visitation in Yosemite Valley doubled, leading to crowding at the Arch Rock Entrance Station.

Yosemite Valley Railroad exhibit, El Portal.

The annoyed driver snapped, "When's the road going to open?" Incredulous, Dick glanced at the man, then at the 30-foot-high boulder, then back at the man. The sound of rain pelting the metal roof pierced the night. "Six weeks, sir. If you care to wait, please make sure your car is pulled completely off the pavement."

While Dick's estimate was made in jest, the road was closed for twenty-one days before crews could reopen it for the public!

E-2 to E-3 is 2.5 miles. E-3 will be on your right.

E-3 ARCH ROCK

The Arch Rock Entrance Station is so named for the two boulders that form an arch over the Yosemite Valley–bound lane.

So severe was the crowding in 1927 that the National Park Service created an advisory board to address crowding conditions in Yosemite Valley. The board ultimately determined that park administrative functions should be moved out of the valley and suggested El Portal (about 15 miles west) as a good location. In 1958, the National Park Service designated the El Portal area for administrative use. The Yosemite View Lodge motel complex is privately owned but farther down the highway, the town of El Portal is government owned.

Yosemite Valley Railroad

There is a turnoff worth the visit 3.5 miles from Arch Rock. The terminus of the Yosemite Valley Railroad is located across the street from the U.S. post office in El Portal. Near there you will see a locomotive, a caboose, and a water tower. This particular locomotive was built in 1921 and was used on the Hetch Hetchy Railroad for transporting men and materials to build the O'Shaughnessy Dam across Hetch Hetchy Valley (see **H-4** on page 56). The locomotive was listed on the National Register of Historic places in 1978. There is also a train station there, relocated from the town of Bagby. That townsite is beneath a reservoir today. The train station currently serves as the local Yosemite Conservancy offices.

Big Oak Flat Road

15.6

There is a parking area at the intersection of the El Portal Road and the Big Oak Flat Road where you may stop and read the introduction to this road tour.

The Big Oak Flat Road opened on July 17, 1874, twenty-nine days after the opening of the Coulterville Road, making it the second wagon road into Yosemite Valley. As it turned out, this road became the more popular road into the valley, ultimately contributing to the Coulterville and Yo Semite Turnpike's business failure.

The current road parallels the old road but doesn't get close to the original route inside the park. Part of the old road is still open to cars, though. If you would like to see what it was like to drive along one of the old wagon roads of Yosemite's past, drive into Tamarack Campground from the Tioga Road at **T-2** (see page 62). Today's road leads to California State Highway 120 west through Groveland, Big Oak Flat, and other points west.

The Big Oak Flat Road is so named because it passes through the gold rush town of Big Oak Flat. The town, in turn, was named after a huge oak tree, eleven feet in diameter, that grew on an open area, or flat, about 42 miles from here. The expansive old tree was so revered that the town passed an ordinance to protect it. In spite of that ordinance, some stealthy vandals dug the dirt out from around the roots one night and hauled the dirt away to pan it for gold in secret. The tree died as a result of this greedy act, was charred by a fire in 1863, and toppled a few years later.

The big oak was left lying where it fell and continued to be a source of pride and a symbol of the community some thirty odd years later. In 1900, however, a camper carelessly let his campfire get away from him, and the tree was mostly consumed by the fire. The camper who caused the fire left town in a hurry. A few pieces of that old tree are enshrined in a small roadside exhibit next to a gas station and minimart.

You have to wonder if that venerable old oak would have survived the fires had it not been killed by the midnight miners. Would it still be spreading its leaves to the sun today? Was the value of the gold from the dirt, if any was found, equal to the value of the living tree?

The intersection of El Portal Road and Big Oak Flat Road to **B-1** is 1.9 miles. **B-1** will be on your left.

B-1 THE CASCADES

Two bridges fairly close to each other carry the road above two streams here: Tamarack Creek and Cascade Creek. The two creeks join forces just below these bridges, then leap over a 500-foot cliff, forming a beautiful waterfall. You can see that waterfall from the El Portal Road at **E-1** (see page 42). In spring, the spray from the cascades above the road drifts across both lanes. This is a nice place to stop and enjoy the rushing water. Many people walk across the road without looking, so be extra cautious here.

B-1 to **B-2** is 0.4 mile. **B-2** will be on your right.

B-2 BRIDALVEIL FALL AND MERCED CANYON

A wonderful view of Bridalveil Fall and the Merced Canyon below Yosemite Valley imposes itself here. In the nearly 1 million years since the last glacier carved the canyon below into a broad U-shaped valley, the Merced River has cut farther into the granites, leaving more of a V-shaped profile. Nature continues to change and rearrange the scenery.

B-2 to **B-3** is 0.8 mile. **B-3** will be on your left.

B-3 HALF DOME VIEW

In 1865, the state geologist of California, Josiah Dwight Whitney, of Mount Whitney fame, wrote in a report that Half Dome is "perfectly inaccessible, being probably the only one of the prominent points about the Yosemite which never has

Big Oak Flat Road, circa 1880.

A model of Half Dome at **B-3** allows a sense of its three dimensions.

been, and never will be, trodden by human foot."

Almost immediately, people began looking for a way to prove Whitney wrong. One of them, a Scots immigrant named George Anderson, would try several times. When climbing Half Dome in his boots proved unsuccessful, he tried bare feet. Then he tried wrapping his feet with sackcloth and applying tree sap for a better grip on the granite. The problem with this technique was how to peel his foot loose without losing his balance.

It was ingenuity that finally solved the problem of how to get to the top of Half Dome. Having been a sailor, Anderson was familiar with ropes and wove several into one strong rope that would catch him if he fell. He then used his blacksmith skills to fashion eyebolts to which he could tie the rope. Armed with his rope, a satchel of eyebolts, a rock drill, and hammer, he headed for the northeast shoulder of Half Dome.

Once there, Anderson climbed as high as he could and drilled a hole in the solid rock. He pounded an eyebolt into the hole and tied his rope to it. Then he climbed higher and repeated the process. Higher and higher he went, sometimes climbing a long way before installing another eyebolt, sometimes standing on one eyebolt while drilling the next hole. In this way he climbed the last 900 feet to the top. On October 12, 1875, George could be seen waving the thirty-seven-star American flag atop the formerly "inaccessible" Half Dome.

We all respond to challenges in one way or another. From the time we are babies, we are challenged with making sense of the world around us. We are physically challenged from our first clumsy steps to our last. The challenge may be physical, intellectual, or emotional. Yosemite challenges us in many ways. It's up to you to meet with challenge in your own way.

B-3 to B-4 is 0.5 mile. B-4 will be on your left.

B-4 EL CAPITAN TRAILHEAD

This parking area is for the trail to the top of El Capitan, 10 miles distant. The trail continues on to Yosemite Falls and the high country beyond. If you have the time, 800 miles of trails crisscross Yosemite's wilderness.

The A-Rock Fire Complex

August 7, 1990, dawned windy and warm just as previous days had, but this day was different. Yosemite was in its third year of drought and as the day passed, storm clouds massed in the sky overhead. At midday, light-

---

Why Would a Tree Want to Catch Fire?

There is a species of pine that lives below the road and to the left at the El Capitan Trailhead, as well as on the ridge in the distance below and to the right of the trailhead. This pine depends on fire for its existence. That's right, it needs fire, and it's well adapted to it. The knobcone pine sprouts and grows very quickly after a fire. Within three years, it bears fertile cones that will remain closed and on the tree until the next fire burns it and causes the cones to open with the heat. Seeds fall from the partially burnt cones almost immediately after the fire passes, and they sprout the following spring. Thus fire provides the passionate flames needed for the knobcone pine to reproduce.

Knobcone pine seedlings grow vigorously after a fire.

ning began striking the western part of the park, igniting multiple fires in the area below you. Within a few hours, a dozen firefighters battled the flames, but to no avail. Three days later, the National Park Service evacuated visitors from Yosemite Valley and closed all three roads into it.

Fanned by 50-mile-an-hour winds, several fires grew together, creating a firestorm that raged through the community of Foresta below. Flames 150 feet high hissed and rumbled through trees and homes alike. The fire raced up the hill past here, jumped the road, and flamed its way to the top of the mountain with explosive force. The fire was finally contained on August 20, and Yosemite Valley reopened. It had been closed for ten days. For more on the A-Rock Complex fires, see **W-3** on page 86.

B-4 to B-5 is 5.8 miles. B-6 will be on your right.

B-5 CRANE FLAT

Crane Flat is situated near the top of the lower montane zone (see pages 18–19 for more on life zones). In this zone, you will see such trees as white fir, ponderosa pine, incense-cedar, and sugar pine. But because the climate is cooler here than at other locations at this elevation, you will see trees typical of higher elevations like red fir and lodgepole pine. The many meadows (also called "flats") here display a brilliant palette of wildflowers. They also provide a dining room for black bears in early summer. Because bears (and other wildlife) rarely look both ways before crossing, the speed limit here is 25 miles per hour. Please drive slowly, even though it may seem tedious.

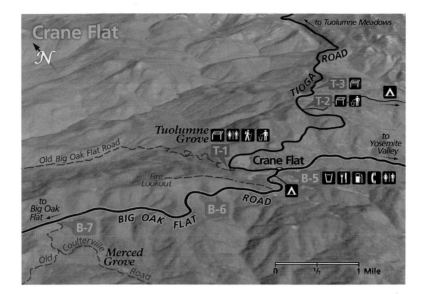

Up the road about 1 mile is a parking area for the trail to the Tuolumne Grove of Giant Sequoias. There is a primitive restroom there as well. A small convenience store and gas station at the intersection of the Big Oak Flat and Tioga Roads also provide restrooms. If you are continuing on Tioga Road, turn to page 63.

B-5 to B-6 is 1.4 miles. B-6 will be on your left.

American black bear eating grass and wildflower plants in Crane Flat Meadow.

Group of six giant sequoias in the Merced Grove.

B-6 SAN JOAQUIN VALLEY OVERLOOK

On a clear day, you can see across the San Joaquin Valley to the Coast Range, over a hundred miles from here. Clear days aren't as common as they once were. The growth of cities in the San Joaquin creates more and more air pollution, which combines with fouled air blown in from the San Francisco Bay Area. This results in loss of visibility as well as damage to trees in the national parks of the Sierra. It's important to understand that many threats to our national parks come from far away.

B-6 to B-7 is 2.3 miles. B-7 will be on your left.

B-7 MERCED GROVE OF GIANT SEQUOIAS

The 3-mile round trip to the Merced Grove descends 600 feet. It follows a dirt road for .6 mile, where it joins the Coulterville Road, the first wagon road to Yosemite Valley, and continues .9 mile to the Grove see page 48. Originally the Coulterville Road had been built to Crane Flat, but when the Merced Grove was rediscovered, the road builders decided it would be more profitable for the road to pass through a giant sequoia grove. For more information about giant sequoias, see pages 93–97.

B-7 to B-8 is 3.9 miles. B-8 will be on your right.

B-8 BIG OAK FLAT ENTRANCE STATION

🔺 🚰 ⓘ 🏪 🏠 👫 🚶

Hodgdon Meadow, about 1 mile away, is named after Jeremiah Hodgdon, who settled there in 1865. In addition to using the meadow as a summer cattle camp, he accommodated and fed travelers on their way to Yosemite Valley. In her book *Bits of Travel at Home* (1878), Helen Hunt Jackson described her experience luxuriating at this fine establishment:

Three, four, five in a room; some on floors, without even a blanket. A few pampered ones, women, with tin pans for wash-bowls and one towel for six hands. The rest, men, with one tin basin in an open shed, and if they had any towel or not I do not know. That was a night at Hogdin's [sic].

Food? Yes. Junks of beef floating in bowls of fat, junks of ham ditto, beans ditto, potatoes as hard as bullets, corn-bread steaming with saleratus, doughnuts ditto, hot biscuits ditto;

the whole set out in indescribable confusion and dirt, in a narrow, unventilated room, dimly lit by two reeking kerosene lamps. Even brave and travelled souls could not help being appalled at the situation.

. . . There was something uncommonly droll in the energetic promptness and loudness with which the landlady roused all her guests at half-past four in the morning.

"You don't suppose we were asleep, do you?" called out somebody, whose sense of humor had not been entirely extinguished by hunger and no bed.

Seriously Helen. What did you *really* think of the place?

A small information center here provides opportunities to talk to rangers, get wilderness permits, or buy books during the summer season. A nearby campground provides a base of operations for exploring Hetch Hetchy, the Merced and Tuolumne groves of giant sequoias, and the western areas of Yosemite National Park.

Hetch Hetchy Road

8.4

If you are traveling to Hetch Hetchy, take the first road (Evergreen Road) to the right about 1 mile west of the park exit on the Big Oak Flat Road (Highway 120). Follow it 7.5 miles to the T intersection, and turn right. The Hetch Hetchy Entrance Station will be another 1.4 miles.

H-1 HETCH HETCHY RANGER STATION

Stop at the Hetch Hetchy Entrance Station, where rangers will issue a day use pass. Backpackers will receive overnight passes. The road into the Hetch Hetchy Reservoir is subject to closure for security measures at any time, and access is limited to daylight hours. Call the information line to find out exact times: (209) 372-0200.

Please be aware that bicyclists also need day use passes, and when the gate is closed, the area is closed to all vehicles, even bikes. Vehicles left unattended after hours may be towed at the owner's expense.

Symbolic Valley

Take a Yosemite-like valley, shrink it to two-thirds size, fill it with water, and what do you get? A symbol of the struggle between the proponents of pragmatic use and the proponents of preservation of national park lands and resources.

What is the purpose of national parks? Should they serve utilitarian needs or should they be preserved as reminders of a wild America for the sake of aesthetics, recreation, and science? Within eleven years after Yosemite National Park was created in 1890, the city of San Francisco proposed to dam the Tuolumne River and flood Hetch Hetchy Valley for a source of water and power. The city's initial efforts failed, but perseverance prevailed.

There was no National Park Service at the time, and the purpose of the national parks wasn't fully realized. However, there were two predominant champions for competing parkland use: John Muir, considered by many to be the father of national

Tuolumne River water flows over the O'Shaughnessy Dam spillway.

parks, and Gifford Pinchot, father of the U.S. Forest Service.

Pinchot believed that all public land should be used for the greatest benefit to the greatest number of people, while Muir felt the national parks should be held under an inviolable concept of preservation. With the passing of the Raker Act on December 19, 1913, Congress gave San Francisco the right to dam Hetch Hetchy and use the Tuolumne River for the city's practical purposes.

Hetch Hetchy reminds us that the preservation of national park lands may not be forever, yet it symbolizes the beginnings of the congressionally mandated national park mission, to preserve park resources for future generations to enjoy. If the same issue were to come up today, where might you stand?

H-1 to H-2 is 1.5 miles. H-2 will be on your right.

H-2 POOPENAUT PASS

The gap you see from here is called Poopenaut Pass, and just ahead you will see O'Shaughnessy Dam and the Hetch Hetchy Reservoir from a distance. The fogs of time and history obscure the meaning of "Poopenaut," but two explanations stand out. One indicates it's the name of an early settler. The other suggests that it is the Indian name for a celery-like plant eaten by the local people. The correct pronunciation may be found in two alternate spellings: Poopino and Poopeno.

A 1-mile trail that leads to the bottom makes sense of another pronunciation. It descends 1,275 feet in 1 mile and takes about 15 minutes. The return trip, taking four times longer, defines the trail known locally as "The Poopin' Out Trail."

If you are surefooted and in good shape, you can get a broad view of the local countryside by carefully climbing up the rock outcrop across the street and to the left.

H-2 to H-3 is 3.5 miles. H-3 will be on your left. Remember to be careful when crossing the oncoming lane of traffic.

H-3 POOPENAUT VALLEY VIEW

There is a picnic table here, where you may wish to enjoy a snack with a view of Poopenaut Valley below.

Poopenaut Valley includes a low-elevation wetland that requires periodic flooding to maintain its health. Having a dam upstream tends to moderate the river flow, so agreements between the National Park Service and the city of San Francisco have been made to release enough water to flood the meadow now and again. Research is underway to determine just how much flooding is necessary to maintain natural conditions in this low-elevation wetland.

If you need water or restrooms, they are 2.5 miles ahead. Look for them on the right once you've passed the residences (please do not disturb them).

H-3 to H-4 is 3.4 miles. H-4 will be on your right.

H-4 HETCH HETCHY RESERVOIR

Parking is just ahead.

What's in a reservoir besides water? In this reservoir, drowned by all that water, are stumps of oak trees that once spread their limbs in the sunlight and sprouted leaves that fluttered in fresh summer breezes. They are stumps of oak trees that once provided homes for woodpeckers, great horned owls, and orioles, as well as food for squirrels, deer, and bears.

View of Poopenaut Valley from H-3.

In this reservoir, drowned by all that water, are the haunts of generations upon generations of American Indians who lived out their lives between the waterfalls and cliffs. They were Indians who named those waterfalls and cliffs and who made food from the acorns dropped by the oaks.

Clearly something special was lost with the filling of this reservoir, but that is not all that was lost. The lives of dozens of workers building the dam were lost as well, mostly from falls or from falling rock or accidents with heavy equipment. At the time, the loss of 1,895 acres of wild lands, the deaths of workers, and $12.6 million were the cost of progress. So how has this progress benefited us today?

The Hetch Hetchy system produces 1.6 billion kilowatts of clean energy each year without burning a molecule of fossil fuel. This energy powers San Francisco as well as the Turlock and Modesto Irrigation Districts. Its gravity-fed system delivers water to 2.5 million San Francisco Bay Area residents. Some say the Hetch Hetchy project led to a stronger sense of the value of our national parks.

A Wonderful Wildflower Walk

Springtime arrives here in April or May, and a walk along the trail across the dam is a delight. The ground is moist, and there are pools that dry in summer. A lush green covers the ground between rocky outcrops, and splashes of color wet the landscape.

As you walk, watch for purple flowers of bush lupine or the lavender-tinged white blossoms of yerba santa, "the herb of the saints." Look for yellow-orange flowers of the succulent dudleya living in cracks in the rocks and pinstriped yellow petals of pretty face growing in dry soil. You may see pink shooting stars dangling above wet places, blue harvest

Yerba Santa blooms on the edge of Hetch Hetchy Reservoir.

Bush lupine in full blossom at Hetch Hetchy.

brodiaea in dried areas, or expanses of goldfields.

At that time of year, you may hear the songs of Pacific tree frogs and find California newts migrating to or from pools where they mate and lay eggs. If you walk far enough, you will come to two waterfalls. The nearest is the tall, straight Tueeulala Falls, and the farthest is Wapama Falls.

Both are Indian names, the meanings of which has been lost. Please be particularly careful about high water. People have lost their lives trying to cross the stream when water is on the bridge.

To return to the Hetch Hetchy Entrance Station, continue up the one road through the parking area and follow the road signs back.

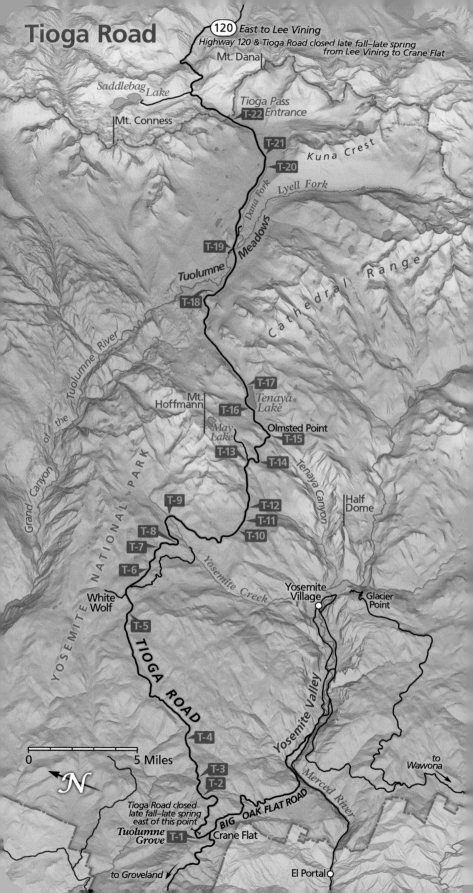

Tioga Road

120 East to Lee Vining
Highway 120 & Tioga Road closed late fall–late spring
from Lee Vining to Crane Flat

Mt. Dana

Saddlebag Lake

Tioga Pass
Entrance
T-22

Mt. Conness

Kuna Crest

T-21

T-20

Dana Fork

Lyell Fork

T-19

Tuolumne Meadows

Cathedral Range

T-18

Tuolumne River

Mt.
Hoffmann

T-17
Tenaya Lake

T-16

Olmsted Point

May Lake

T-15

T-13

T-14

Grand Canyon

Tenaya Canyon

YOSEMITE NATIONAL PARK

of the

T-9

T-12

T-11

T-10

Half
Dome

T-8

T-7

T-6

Yosemite Creek

Yosemite Village

Glacier
Point

White
Wolf

T-5

Yosemite Valley

TIOGA ROAD

T-4

to
Wawona

T-3

T-2

Merced River

0   5 Miles

N

Tioga Road closed
late fall–late spring
east of this point

Tuolumne
Grove

BIG OAK FLAT ROAD

T-1

Crane Flat

to Groveland

El Portal

Tioga Road

42.2 mls

The Tioga Road begins where it intersects with the Big Oak Flat Road at Crane Flat. To read about Crane Flat, see **B-5** on page 52.

Tioga Road is a pathway of history, scenic wonder, and biological diversity. Beginning at Crane Flat (6,192 ft.), Tioga Road climbs through forests of pine and fir interspersed with meadows, lakes, and rocky outcrops to an elevation close to 8,000 feet in about 10 miles. From there it undulates along mountains and valleys with spectacular views of Yosemite's high country.

Forty miles from here, at 8,600 feet elevation, Tuolumne Meadows, a wide-open garden with panoramic vistas of ice-sculpted mountains and domes, comes into view.

Then the road climbs 1,300 feet in about 10 miles, through subalpine forests and meadows to Tioga Pass (9,943 ft.), where peaks soar thousands of feet higher. Finally the highway descends 3,000 feet down the steep eastern escarpment of the Sierra Nevada to the high deserts of eastern California.

The earliest people to cross these mountains followed animal trails. Eventually these American Indians established trade routes. Later, mountain men, miners, sheepherders, and explorers followed those paths.

Immigrant workers, from as far away as China, built the original Tioga Road. After Yosemite National Park was created, cavalry soldiers, civilian rangers, and then National Park Service rangers patrolled the area. Today, visitors from all over the world cross the Sierra Nevada along this route, and now you may count yourself among those who have passed this way for thousands of years.

If you drive carefully, you can make the trip in a couple of hours, while early travelers took days.

From the intersection of the Tioga Road with the Big Oak Flat Road to T-1 is 0.5 mile. T-1 will be on your left.

Tioga Road wends through the high country of Yosemite.

T-1 TUOLUMNE GROVE OF GIANT SEQUOIAS

The old Big Oak Flat Road passes through the Tuolumne Grove about 1 mile from here. That old road is closed to cars, but the walk along it is enjoyable and will take about 30 minutes going down and about 1 hour coming back up. This is because it's a loss of 500 feet in elevation going down and a gain of 500 feet in elevation coming back up.

There are fine specimens in this small grove, including a 60-foot-high stump

Tuolumne Grove's Dead Giant.

with a tunnel that was cut through it in 1878 for tourists to enjoy. For further information on giant sequoias, see pages 93-97.

T-1 to T-2 is 3.2 miles. T-2 will be on your right.

T-2 GIN FLAT

An old Indian trail called the Mono Trail passes near here and parallels the Tioga Road. It is one segment of a network of American Indian trade routes that led from the Pacific Ocean across the mountains of California and far beyond. Many people traded buffalo robes, originating in the distant east, westward along these trails to the Pacific Ocean. Seashells and beads changed hands along the route equally far in the opposite direction.

These old trails may have their beginnings long before humans ever lived in the Americas. At first, animals made trails as they roamed. Some researchers suggest there may even be sections of Indian trails in the lowlands that were originally made by migrating mastodons. Imagine that! The very first human explorers in the Americas had intimate knowledge of such ice age animals as woolly

People have been making tracks across the Sierra for thousands of years.

mammoths, giant ground sloths, and saber-toothed cats. While this may be speculation, we know for sure the people have been living in the Yosemite region for at least 8,000 years.

T-2 to T-3 is 0.9 mile. T-3 will be on your right.

T-3 WALKER PARTY

In 1833, Joseph Reddeford Walker led a party of half-starved mountain men across the Sierra. After two weeks of struggling through snow, one member of the party, Zenas Leonard, wrote in his journal:

We spent no time in idleness—scarcely stopping in our journey to view an occasional specimen of the wonders of nature's handy work. . . We traveled a few miles every day . . . obliged to keep along the top of the dividing ridge between two of these chasms which seemed to lead pretty near in the direction we were going.

You are on that dividing ridge! Imagine how you might have felt if you were traveling with explorers. The journal continues:

. . . the vigour of every man almost exhausted   nothing to give our poor

horses, which were no longer any assistance to us in traveling, but a burthen, for we had to help the most of them along as we would an old and feeble man.

It seemed to be the greatest cruelty to take your rifle, when your horse sinks to the ground from starvation, but still manifests a desire and willingness to follow you, to shoot him in the head and then cut him up & take such parts of their flesh as extreme hunger alone will render it possible for a human being to eat. This we done several times, and it was the only thing that saved us from death. 24 of our horses died since we arrived on top of the mountain—17 of which we eat the best parts.

ZENAS LEONARD, 1833, IN
*NARRATIVE OF THE ADVENTURES
OF ZENAS LEONARD*

Consider this: Right now you could drive to Yosemite Valley and buy a sandwich within about an hour. If you chose to head east and cross the mountains, you could have a meal in less than two.

Joseph Reddeford Walker's headstone in Martinez, California.

Sunset at Sunset View.

How lucky we are today to drive comfortably in climate-controlled vehicles on smooth, paved roads, stopping as often and for as long as we like to view specimens "of the wonders of nature's handy-work."

T-3 to T-4 is 0.9 mile. T-4 will be on your right.

T-4 SUNSET VIEW

The sun sets beyond the Coast Range 100 miles west of here. You can see these mountains on a clear day, but clear days aren't as common as they once were. Most other places in Yosemite where people enjoy the daily miracle don't afford a view to the west. People watch the colors change on Half Dome or the high mountains of the Sierra crest. Here you can watch the sun actually dip into the distant horizon.

The view here takes in the lower reaches of the South Fork of the Tuolumne River watershed. Drive 1.8 miles from here, and the road crosses the river on a small bridge. Like many watercourses in Yosemite, it dries up each year as snow from the previous winter melts away.

T-4 to T-5 is 7.9 miles. T-5 will be on your right.

T-5 SIESTA LAKE

At 8,200 feet in elevation, this quiet pond provides us with evidence of a glacier that once flowed here. Imagine standing on the rocky hill across the road 20,000 years ago in late summer, looking toward where the lake is now. Right at your feet would be blue-tinted ice at the bottom of a glacier stretching up to an alcove in the mountain to the left. The upper part of the glacier would be covered with white snow strewn with dirt, rocks, and boulders fallen from the cliffs above.

If you were to look closely at the ice, you might see pebbles at the bottom of water-filled tubes in the ice. Dark stones absorb the energy from the rays of the sun. The energy in the light warms the little rocks, which, in turn, melt the ice. In this way they keep melting their way deeper and deeper into the glacier. You would hear the sound of meltwater gurgling through the rocks off to the right.

The Formation of Siesta Lake

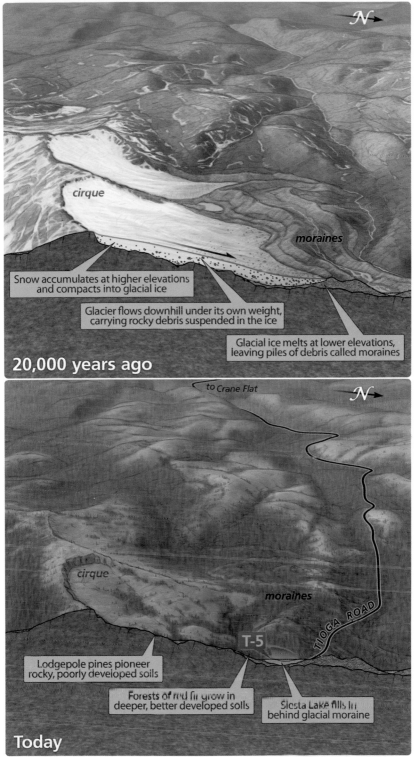

cirque

moraines

Snow accumulates at higher elevations
and compacts into glacial ice

Glacier flows downhill under its own weight,
carrying rocky debris suspended in the ice

Glacial ice melts at lower elevations,
leaving piles of debris called moraines

20,000 years ago

to Crane Flat

cirque

moraines

TIOGA ROAD

T-5

Lodgepole pines pioneer
rocky, poorly developed soils

Forests of red fir grow in
deeper, better developed soils

Siesta Lake fills in
behind glacial moraine

Today

A glacier is a mass of ice that flows under its own weight. Glaciers pluck chunks of rock from the side of the mountain where the glacier began. Eventually this action creates a cirque (a rocky bowl, or amphitheater-like structure). Rocks also fall onto the glacier. These rocks ride in and on the ice as it flows and slides down the mountain, and they provide the tools for the glacier to carve away at the bedrock that it moves over.

At some point, the ice flows far enough down the mountain to where the climate is warm enough for the snow and ice to melt. As the ice melts, the glacier's load of rocks, sand, gravel, and grit drop out. When the snout of the glacier is low enough for the ice to melt back as fast as it is flowing forward, rocks are exposed and dropped into a pile called a "moraine."

A glacier is like a conveyor belt carrying rock from high in the mountains to the lower valleys. In the case of this glacier, the glacial conveyer belt was only about 1 mile long, whereas the glaciers in Hetch Hetchy and Yosemite Valley were 20 to 30 miles long. The cirque where the Siesta Glacier was born is the westernmost cirque in the Sierra Nevada.

That rocky hill where you imagine yourself standing is the moraine, and a glacier piled it there. The illustrations on page 67 help show how the scene came to be as it is today. After the glaciers melted, a lake formed behind the moraine, and plants colonized the land. That is what happened here at Siesta Lake, but that's not the end of the story. Plants will continue to grow in and around the lake as dust, sand, and gravel wash into the water. In this way, the lake will fill with soil and become a meadow. That is what is happening right now.

White Wolf

About 1 mile from here is the turnoff for White Wolf, a small, rustic resort made up of a few cabins and a dining room where breakfast and dinner are served during the summer season. The resort and the nearby campground are set amid lodgepole pine forests growing among several meadows.

Shooting star at White Wolf.

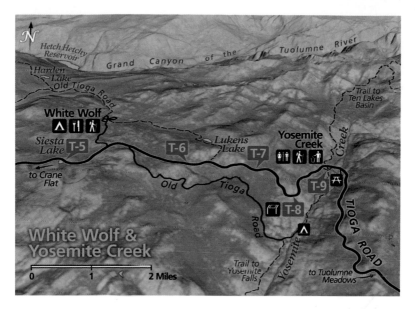

White Wolf & Yosemite Creek

0   1   2 Miles

At the campground, rangers provide guided walks and campfire talks. A stretch of the old Tioga Road serves as a trail to Harden Lake, with connecting trails into the Tuolumne River canyon and back to the campground. Another trail meanders up to Lukens Lake, about 2.3 miles distant.

Yosemite Creek Campground

Just beyond the turnoff to White Wolf, on the right is the road to primitive Yosemite Creek Campground. The 3-mile road to the campground follows the original route of the old Tioga Road.

T-5 to T-6 is 2.3 miles. T-6 will be on your right.

T-6 MCSWAIN SUMMIT

At 8,300 feet in elevation, McSwain Summit marks a divide between the Merced and Tuolumne Rivers. To the north and west, water flows into the Tuolumne. To the south and east, water flows into the Merced. The soils just west of here on northern slopes provide ideal growing conditions for red fir trees. In fact, one of

the red fir trees in that forest holds the record for being the largest tree of its species. The headwaters of the Middle Fork of the Tuolumne River originate, in part, on the slopes slightly north and west of here.

The terrain south and east of here becomes rockier, with generally shallower soils on south-facing slopes, which tend to be dryer than northern slopes. You are likely to see trees like Jeffrey pine and western juniper in these thirsty locations.

White fir, found usual below 6,500 feet, grow in a few places 1,500 feet above their usual range, illustrating just one of many exceptions to the generalized life zones explained on pages 18-19.

T-6 to T-7 is 0.6 mile. T-7 will be on your right.

T-7 CLARK RANGE VIEW

Many people refer to the Sierra Nevada as the Sierras. The original name given this mountain range by Spanish explorers was Una Gran Sierra Nevada. This translates to "A Great Snowy Mountain Range." So,

| Cloud's Rest (not part of the Clark Range) | Mount Clark | Gray Peak | Red Peak | Merced Peak |

Clark Range.

technically, the name is singular. In fact, many historians harp on this vigorously.

On the other hand, there are numerous groups of peaks that collectively bear the name range. Such is the case with the Clark Range. The view of the Clark Range from this 8,200-foot viewpoint is wonderful and complete. Mount Clark bears the name of Yosemite's—and the world's—first park ranger, Galen Clark. See his story at **G-5** on page 103.

T-7 to T-8 is 1.6 miles. T-8 will be on your right.

T-8 YOSEMITE CREEK VIEW

Scan the landscape all around this point. Everything you see is within the Yosemite Creek watershed. The highest point, Mount Hoffmann (10,850 ft.), rises to the east. The lowest point on the horizon to the south is near where all the water that flows out of this basin leaps some 2,400 feet into Yosemite Valley as Yosemite Falls. Note how much bedrock shows. Even where you see forests, the soils are fairly gravelly and shallow, so they don't hold much groundwater. When the snow in this basin has melted, the creek ceases to flow. And so do Yosemite Falls.

T-8 to T-9 is 1.4 miles. T-9 will be on your right.

T-9 YOSEMITE CREEK

Yosemite Creek drains this area, as well as the many smaller creeks that run off the surrounding mountains, the highest of which is Mount Hoffmann. The creek consists entirely of snowmelt, and when the snow has

Quaking Aspen (*Populus tremuloides*)

What a beautiful tree! Its smooth white trunk supports a riot of tremulous leaves that flutter wildly in the mountain breezes. The quaking aspen is one of few deciduous trees at these higher elevations, and it has an equally beautiful adaptation to conditions here, where evergreen conifers dominate the cold, snowy climes.

When the leaves are gone, the quaking aspen retains green chlorophyll just under its thin white bark. This way, when the snows begin to melt and groundwater is available, it can use the power of sunlight to make sugars from water in the ground and carbon dioxide in the air. This gives the quaking aspen a head start on food production as soon as it is warm enough for its sap to flow.

Quaking aspen leaf and bark.

completely gone, it's a matter of a few days for the last of the water to trickle down to the cliff where the magnificent springtime Yosemite Falls once bellowed their mountain mantra. The reason for the great change in the voice of Yosemite Falls is that the entire watershed of Yosemite Creek is on south-facing slopes, which dry out rapidly in the spring and summer sun.

A peaceful picnic area across the creek is accessible to cars a short distance east of the bridge that crosses the creek.

Yosemite Falls Trail

A trail to the top of Yosemite Falls, Yosemite Valley, and the north rim of the Valley begins here. It parallels the watercourse down to Yosemite Creek Campground on the old Tioga Road, mentioned at **T-5** on page 69. From there it continues 6 miles more to the top of Yosemite Falls.

On the north side of the road, the trail climbs up to the Ten Lakes Basin, a beautiful subalpine area near the slopes of 11,000-foot peaks.

You don't have to walk for miles and miles. If you just want to stretch your legs for a few minutes, you can simply saunter along the trail for a while and turn back whenever you like. There is always something to see, be it a chipmunk, a wildflower, or maybe a bear.

T-9 to T-10 is 4.1 miles. T-10 will be on your right.

T-10 PORCUPINE FLAT

An 1863 map labels this area as Porcupine Flat, but the originator of the name seems to be lost in the folds of history. Porcupines are not at all common here today.

Another wildlife species—said to be more abundant here than anywhere else in the park 100 years ago—is no longer here. Sierra yellow-legged frogs are completely absent from the area today. We have reasonably good evidence that the frogs are dying out, in part because of a fungus (*Batrachochytrium dendrobatidis*). The fungus infects certain skin cells, making it difficult for the frogs to breathe, drink, and take up needed minerals through their skin.

Our national parks are places where wildness is protected for us today and for future generations to enjoy. They protect habitat needed for native wildlife. Hopefully, a cure for this new amphibian disease will be found, and Porcupine Flat will once again support a large, healthy population of these native frogs.

Yellow-legged frog.

T-10 to T-11 is 0.5 mile. T-11 will be on your right.

T-11 CONES AND NEEDLES TRAIL

Four trees typical of the upper montane zone grow here. A short path with informative signs provides opportunities to explore these trees as well as learn about their interrelationships with some of the wildlife in the area.

This location is unusual in that the microclimate favors one tree species that ordinarily grows at much lower elevations. The white fir is a component of the lower montane zone, while here we are at the higher edge of the upper montane zone. (For more on life zones, see pages 18-19.) The shape of the mountains contributes greatly to microclimates. Warmer and dryer, this south-facing slope provides a pathway for lower-elevation species to climb the mountains.

But it's not as simple as that! Soil type plays a role as well, and beyond that, there are mysteries yet to be solved. There aren't any good adult specimens of white fir here, but there are some at the next stop.

The large red fir tree down slope to the right was cut because it threatened to fall onto the road. It had lived about two centuries.

Red fir trees.

Imagine a tiny seed fluttering to the ground and sprouting when the United States was young and California was under Spanish rule. Picture the young tree as a 3-foot-high sapling brushing the leg of an American Indian as he walks by on a hunting trip. Sixty or seventy years later, perhaps a Basque shepherd leans briefly against the trunk on this now-young conifer as he herds sheep between meadows.

Then in 1883, a Chinese laborer takes a break from building the original Tioga Road and walks up here to eat lunch in the shade of this tree. In 1890, Yosemite National Park is created, and that 100-year-old tree stands strong and now protected from ax and saw by U.S. Cavalry patrols using the now-abandoned old Tioga Road.

Time passes, and the tree witnesses early tourists, and even the first National Park Service director, Stephen Tyng Mather, and Yosemite's first civilian superintendent, Washington B. "Dusty" Lewis, making a trip across the mountains in 1928.

Surely this tree's limbs shook in the 1960s, when road builders blasted nearby granite to make room for the modern highway you've been driving. Soon after that, one of the authors of the 1961 *Yosemite Road Guide* stood looking at the excellent bole of this great red fir tree and decided to use it as a representative of its species for people to see and learn from.

Two hundred summers and two hundred winters this tree stood. Two hundred springs and two hundred autumns this tree experienced, and now it lies there breaking down into future soil. Cell by cell, the stories of its life dissolve into the past, only to be reanimated in the fertile beds of our imagination.

T-11 to T-12 is 0.5 mile. T-12 will be on your right.

T-12 NORTH DOME TRAIL

Lightning stripped the bark from this white fir.

The large trees directly behind the restrooms are white fir trees growing far above their "normal" range, which on north-facing slopes is just above 6,000 feet. This is because the warmer, drier mountain slope provides suitable habitat for the trees.

T-12 to T-13 is 2.1 miles. T-13 will be on your left.

T-13 MAY LAKE JUNCTION

This is another segment of the Old Tioga Road, originally built by the Great Sierra Consolidated Silver Company at a cost of $64,000 and completed in 1883. It offers a great opportunity to gain a sense of what it might have been like to travel across the Sierra eighty years ago, although

the road was not paved then. The road passes some beautiful country as it snakes through meadows, rocky terrain, and subalpine forests. The detour will take only 15 minutes' driving time and is well worth it. There is a parking area at the end of the road, where you may wish to make the short, steep hike to May Lake at just over 9,330 feet elevation.

Snow Flat

Yosemite provides more than beauty and recreational opportunities. Some 25 million people and more than 1 million acres of farmland in California depend on runoff from Sierra snowmelt, and Yosemite's two major river systems play a large role in capturing and storing that snow. About 1 mile up the road is one of the locations where rangers measure the snow depth once a month during

Mountain Hemlock
(Tsuga mertensiana)

Mountain hemlocks are the ballerinas of the forest. The tops of the trees and their limbs bend gracefully at their tips. Some of the most accessible specimens dance along this road. There are several within 100 feet of you right now.

Mountain hemlock.

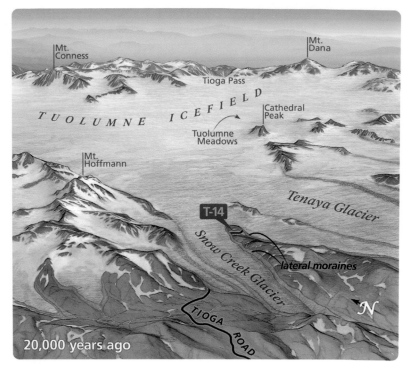

Labels in image: Mt. Conness, Mt. Dana, Tioga Pass, Cathedral Peak, TUOLUMNE ICEFIELD, Tuolumne Meadows, Mt. Hoffmann, Tenaya Glacier, T-14, Snow Creek Glacier, lateral moraines, TIOGA ROAD, 20,000 years ago

T-14 area at the height of the last glaciation.

the winter. These measurements help the California Department of Water Resources calculate how much water will run off the mountains into the Central Valley, where a considerable amount of California's produce is grown. Some of the deepest snows accumulate at Snow Flat.

T-13 to T-14 is 0.5 mile. T-14 will be on your right.

T-14 GLACIAL MORAINE

The hillside west of here is a lateral moraine left by the Snow Creek Glacier. A lateral moraine is a pile of silt, sand, pebbles, rocks, and boulders piled up along the side of a glacier. (See "Geologic Story," page 11.) Had you been here 20,000 years ago, you would have been under the edge of that glacier, which was but a small splinter of the huge river of ice that carved out the Tuolumne gorge and

Hetch Hetchy Valley. This splinter of that glacier flowed down to Tenaya Canyon and into Yosemite Valley.

From here it is about 50 miles to Yosemite Valley by car. You can get there on foot in 8.7 miles.

T-14 to T-15 is 0.5 miles. T-15 will be on your right.

T-15 OLMSTED POINT

The mountains here exhibit a landscape of mostly barren rock. Clouds Rest, Half Dome, and the mountain across the road are granite exposed by millions of years of weathering and erosion. Trees, shrubs, and other plants grow in cracks in the rock, as well as in locations where sand and gravel settle.

Wonderfully sculpted western junipers scattered on the mountain across the road from the parking area remind us of the harsh winters here. Gnarled and stunted, these trees are a part of the subalpine forest, where they grow much taller and straighter than the tortured individuals in this sea of rock. It's not that they like to grow in these dry, windswept scenes. They're just more tolerant of conditions that kill many other species.

Nature Trail

A great little trail here leads to a peaceful spot a short distance from the road and parking area (a quarter of a mile round trip). It passes several picturesque junipers and ends near a very large erratic boulder—a boulder carried by a glacier from its original setting and then dropped as the ice melted.

T-15 to T-16 is 1.7 miles. T-16 will be on your right.

Yellow-bellied marmot.

Yellow-Bellied Marmot

You may encounter some large rodents waddling about, looking cute, and accepting handouts. They are called marmots, but many people mistake them for groundhogs or woodchucks. It's easy to do since the two are closely related. The groundhog's scientific name is *Marmota monax*, while the yellow-bellied marmot's is *Marmota flaviventris*. Please do not feed them or any wildlife you may see in the park.

This weather-beaten western juniper has survived many harsh winters.

Tenaya Lake beckons picnickers and bathers.

T-16 TENAYA LAKE

Tenaya Lake is famous for its glacial polish; that is, rocks that a glacier burnished to a smooth luster. Even 14,000 years later, these rocks reflect the warm light of the setting sun. Local American Indians called the lake Py-we-ack, meaning "shining rocks." This polish can be found at the foot of Polly Dome, on the north side of the lake and the road.

Stop and take a close look at the polish. Look closely, and you will find fine scratches, or striations, that run parallel to one another. These striations were made by bits of sand embedded in the ice like sand on sandpaper. As the glacier moved forward, it "sanded" the rock. Stria-

tions show the direction the glacier traveled.

Tenaya Peak

The prominent mountain that rises above the south shore (opposite the road) of the lake is Tenaya Peak (10,301 ft.). It also bears evidence of glaciation. Note the large amphitheater, or bowl, on the near side of the peak. That is a cirque made at the headwaters of a glacier that plucked rock from the side of the mountain. Reaching its maximum size about 20,000 years ago, this small glacier contributed to the ice that traveled all the way down to Yosemite Valley. Some of the rock from here can perhaps be found in the terminal and recessional moraines west of El Capitan. (See page 15 for a discussion of the different types of glacial moraines.)

Mysterious Tree Trunks Sticking Out of the Lake

Gaze across the water's surface near the northeast part of Tenaya Lake. You will see what look like stumps rising out of the water. If it is early spring, the water may be too high for

A tree rooted in the bottom of Tenaya Lake represents a very dry climate in the past.

you to see them, but they are there and have been for a long time. These so-called stumps are actually the tops of broken-off tree trunks. Some are 70 feet tall. They were once thought to be debris from past avalanches, but divers found they are actually rooted in what was the shoreline of the lake about 1,000 years ago. This was determined by carbon-dating the wood.

How could this be? The stumps certainly didn't grow underwater! As it turns out, changes in climate have brought on some extremely long-term droughts in California's past— droughts that lasted from many decades to centuries. Evidence from other areas, including Mono Lake and the Lake Tahoe area, appears to show the same thing. It was so dry in the past that the lake level dropped as much as 70 feet—long enough for trees to sprout and grow that tall.

This evidence of a radically different climate in the past may be a prologue to a drastically different climate in the future. No one can know for sure, but it is certainly something to consider.

Picnicking

There are many places where people can enjoy lunch near the lake. If you are looking for a place to barbecue hot dogs or marshmallows, or if you just want a fire, you must use designated locations and fire pits.

T-16 to T-17 is 1.0 miles. T-17 will be on your right.

T-17 TENAYA BEACH

In midsummer, once the lake level drops, a gleaming white sandy beach along the east end of the lake invites picnickers and bathers alike.

Lodgepole Pine Forest

You have left the upper montane forests behind. (For more on Yosemite's life zones, see pages 18-19.) From here to Tioga Pass, the forests are made up almost entirely of lodgepole pines.

Diversity of life provides for stability of life. The montane forests of Yosemite are a mix of many species of trees. If one species has a crop failure, animals dependent on its seeds can switch to other species. It's unusual to find large expanses of a single species of tree, and yet here we are in a forest made up almost entirely of lodgepole pine trees, and you will see these lodgepole pine forests all the way to Tioga Pass. Yosemite has vast expanses of subalpine forests made up of lodgepole pine, which can be dangerous to the trees themselves, for it makes them susceptible to disease outbreaks.

Lodgepole pine cone.

One organism that can wipe out widespread tracts of these forests is the needle miner moth. The caterpillar hatches and begins to bore into a lodgepole pine needle. It eats the central part of the needle, and when it has mined its way from one end to the other, it exits the needle, bores into another, and continues its mining activity. In the life of one caterpillar, a needle miner can kill three to five needles.

When conditions are favorable, the population of needle miner moths explodes and infests mile upon square mile of lodgepole pine forest. Even at the rate of only three to five needles per each caterpillar, entire forests can be defoliated. Imagine driving through forests of reddish-brown trees. Now imagine walking through one of these forests when the moths are flying. The moths are light colored and fairly small, and when they all fly at once, they look like millions of snowflakes drifting through the trees. It's really a fantastic scene.

Fortunately, the trees can take being defoliated two or three times without being killed. If the outbreak continues, however, the trees will eventually die, leaving widespread areas of "ghost forest" where all the mature trees are dead. This cycle has been going on for a very long time. The moths and the trees are native to the area, and nature has seen fit to allow both to survive. Young trees survive for some reason and eventually grow to replace the ghosts.

The National Park Service once sprayed vast areas with insecticides to kill off the needle miner moths, even though many other "beneficial" insects died as a result. A change in management policies was codified in 1980. Since then, Yosemite's policy has been to "allow natural processes to prevail," and the needle miner's activities are considered a natural process just as natural fire and thunderstorms are considered part of the natural processes that support life in Yosemite.

T-17 to T-18 is 4.9 miles. T-18 will be on your left.

Erratic boulders atop Pothole Dome.

T-18 TUOLUMNE MEADOWS

Tuolumne Meadows is one of the largest subalpine meadow complexes in the Sierra Nevada, extending 10 miles up the Lyell Fork of the Tuolumne River. Some books may tell you the area was not explored until Euro-American posses and miners came on the scene in the mid-1800s, but that is pretty far from actual fact. Indian people explored every nook and cranny of these mountains long before anyone from the outside world set foot on the North American continent. Tuolumne Meadows was a central meeting point for American Indian people from either side of the mountains as early as 4,500 years ago.

Tuolumne Meadows is a jumping-off point to Yosemite's vast wilderness. Trails lead toward all points of the compass and connect with 800 miles of various other trails. More of an outpost, there is little here in the way of modern comforts.

Pothole Dome

The dome across this little piece of Tuolumne Meadows is called Pothole Dome because fast-moving water made potholes on the south side of the dome. But get this—the water flowed uphill when those potholes were made. How can that be? The water was confined in a tunnel beneath a glacier and flowed from a point much higher. Thus it flowed under pressure up and over the dome in the same way that water can flow uphill in a garden hose. The potholes formed when stones, whirled in circles in an eddy, scoured basins in the bedrock.

A trail, paralleling the road from the turnout at the west end of Tuolumne Meadows, leads to the dome, where you may explore other glacial features

Autumn in Tuolumne Meadows.

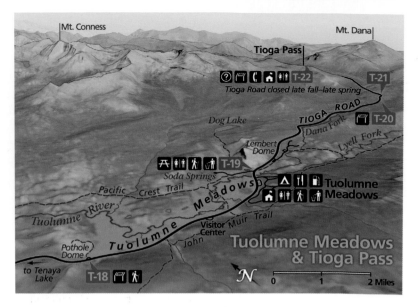

like glacier polish (rock burnished smooth by glaciers), striations (parallel scratches on glacial polish), and erratic boulders (boulders carried, then dropped by a melting glacier). It's an easy climb of about 200 feet up the gently sloping east side of Pothole Dome to the top, where the view of Tuolumne Meadows and its surroundings is inspirational.

The dome itself is one big glacial feature called a "roche moutonnée," formed when glaciers rode up the gentle eastern slope and then plucked or pulled away rocks from the western or downstream slope. There are fanciful stories about the technical name for this kind of formation, which translates as "sheep rock," referring to the shape of a sheep with its head down as it grazes. The gentle slope is the neck of the sheep, and the precipitous side is the sheep's rear end.

Facilities at Tuolumne Meadows

Rangers welcome you at the visitor center, where you may peruse the exhibits, ask questions, or buy maps and books. A campground with 300-plus campsites provides a semiwild experience in a lodgepole pine forest. The concessioner puts up a large tent each summer that houses a market, a post office, and a grill. Tuolumne Meadows Lodge is also made up of tents. One large tent houses the dining hall, registration, and lounge, and about sixty-nine metal-framed canvas tents serve as rooms. The stables provide tours of the area as well as transportation into the wilderness. There is also a gas station.

T-18 to T-19 is 2.4 miles. T-19 will be on your left.

T-19 LEMBERT DOME

The nearly 900-foot-high dome here is a roche moutonnée named after homesteader Jean (John) Baptiste Lembert.

Dog Lake

This is a relatively warm lake with a fairly short trail to it (1.4 miles). It's great for families. With kids, make a scavenger hunt or a game that gets them looking farther up the trail, and they'll be at the lake in no time.

Lembert Dome, a roche moutonnée. Glaciers flowed from right to left, smoothing the gentle slope and plucking rock from the cliff.

Soda Springs

There is a level 1-mile walk on the gravel road to Soda Springs, where Jean Baptiste Lembert's homestead was. At the springs, carbonated water bubbles up out of the ground.

In 1889, John Muir took Robert Underwood Johnson, editor of the *Century Magazine*, to Tuolumne Meadows so Johnson could see how sheep were damaging the land. Muir convinced Johnson that the area could only be saved if it was incorporated into a national park. They camped at Soda Springs, where Johnson suggested that Muir write two magazine articles describing the beauty of the area and the damage to that beauty, and proposing a national park.

Johnson's publication of Muir's exposés in August and September of 1890 sparked a bill in the U.S. Congress that proposed creating a new federally administered park surrounding the old Yosemite Grant. Yosemite National Park became a reality in October 1890.

Cathedral Range

On the south side of the meadows, a series of mountains between the Merced and Tuolumne rivers makes up the Cathedral Range. Cathedral Peak (10,911 ft.), perhaps the

Soda Springs.

The Cathedral Range, with Unicorn Peak on the left and Cathedral Peak on the right.

most striking of the range, was first climbed by John Muir. After he climbed it, he noted in his journal that it was the first time he had attended church since arriving in California. Unicorn Peak (10,823 ft.), named for its fancied likeness to a unicorn from a certain angle, is the next major peak to the east of Cathedral Peak. Then comes Johnson Peak (11,040 ft.), which is made up of the youngest granites in Yosemite.

T-19 to T-20 is 4.1 miles. T-20 will be on your right.

T-20 MONO TRAIL

Interpretive exhibits tell about mountain and granite formation and environmental changes to the meadows. From here you can see the gap where the old Mono Trail leads to the high deserts east of the Sierra Nevada. As mentioned earlier (see **T-2** on page 64), this was a trade route for people on either side of the mountains for centuries and perhaps millennia.

In 1990, descendants of native peoples from either side of the mountains began an annual commemorative walk between Yosemite Valley and Walker Lake on the east side of the mountains. Each year, a group of people walks the 35 miles across the mountains as did their ancestors. In ancient times, the crossing was a matter of year-to-year survival of the people. Today the trip promotes the survival of their cultures and tribal identities.

T-20 to T-21 is 1.0 mile. T-21 will be on your right.

T-21 DANA / GIBBS VIEW

Many peaks in the Sierra have names, and many more don't. Three of Yosemite's highest peaks are named after scientists, and two, Mounts Dana and Gibbs, are visible from this point.

Mount Dana, the second highest at 13,053 feet, was climbed and named by members of the Geological Survey of California on June 28, 1863. They gave it the name of the most eminent American geologist, James Dwight Dana, professor of natural history and geology at Yale.

Five days later, they named another peak, along the crest of the Sierra, after the most eminent English geologist, Sir Charles Lyell. Mount Lyell is the highest peak in Yosemite at 13,114 feet.

On August 31, 1864, William Henry Brewer of the Whitney Geological

Dana Fork of the Tuolumne River with the Sierra crest in the background.

Mounts Dana and Gibbs from a picturesque pond.

Survey, and Frederick Law Olmsted, the famous landscape architect of New York's Central Park, climbed to the top of the 12,764-foot Mount Gibbs. Olmsted's feet never touched the ground en route. Why? He rode to the summit on horseback! Olmsted named the peak after Oliver Wolcott Gibbs, a professor of science at Harvard.

T-21 to T-22 is 1.5 miles. T-22 will be on your right.

T-22 DANA MEADOWS

Now, at nearly 10,000 feet, you are near the top of the subalpine zone. These meadows are quite fragile in part because the growing season is

Bennettville, a ghost town near Tioga Pass, is near the original destination of the Tioga Road.

so short. Snow remains as late as July and the first snows of winter often arrive in September. It can freeze any night of the year.

Short Hike to the Arctic

Just a few hundred feet above Dana Meadows, trees can no longer grow because of the shortness of the growing season.

There is a wonderful trail that begins 500 feet up the road at another parking area nearer Tioga Pass. While steep, the trail is only 1 mile long and provides magnificent views of the surrounding countryside. The trail zigs and zags through the last of forests up into the landscape beyond the trees. The high point, about 600 feet above the parking area, rewards with breathtaking views those who ascend the trail.

You can also walk the last mile of the original Tioga Road to the Tioga Mine and ghost town of Bennettville. That trail begins outside the park .9 mile beyond the Tioga Pass Entrance Station.

Tioga Pass

Once you pass through the Tioga Pass Entrance Station at 9,943 feet, you will be out of the park and headed down the east side of the mountains, and within half an hour you will have crossed the Sierra Nevada.

Here ends my forever memorable first High Sierra excursion. I have crossed the Range of Light, surely the brightest and best of all the Lord has built; and rejoicing in its glory, I gladly, gratefully, hopefully pray I may see it again.

JOHN MUIR, IN HIS JOURNAL,
SEPTEMBER 19, 1869

From T-22 to Tioga Pass is 0.1 mile.

Tioga Pass entrance to Yosemite, with Kuna Crest in background.

to Crane Flat

The Cascades

El Capitan

Yosemite Valley

Merced River

W-2

Foresta

W-1

Bridalveil Fall

Bridalveil Creek

to El Portal

W-3

GLACIER POINT ROAD

Yosemite West

Chinquapin

W-4

Badger Pass

Glacier Point Road closed late fall–late spring east of Badger Pass

Bridalveil Creek

Y O S E M I T E

N A T I O N A L   P A R K

South Fork Merced River

W A W O N A   R O A D

Chilnualna Creek

Chilnualna Falls

S I E R R A

N. F.

W-5

W-6

Wawona

W-7

South Fork Merced River

N

W-8

Mariposa Grove

Road closed late fall–late spring

0   1   2 Miles

South Entrance

Wawona Road

41 to Oakhurst & Fresno

Wawona Road

The Wawona Road climbs out of the west end of Yosemite Valley near Bridalveil Fall. To get there, take the one-way road out of Yosemite Valley and follow the signs toward Highway 41 (Fresno). If you are entering the valley from the El Portal Road (Highway 140) or the Big Oak Flat Road (Highway 120), you will also follow signs toward Highway 41 (Fresno).

The Wawona Road opened for business on April 18, 1875, even though a 900-foot section was yet to be completed. Wagons pulled up to the rough section, and passengers got out and walked across. The stage was taken apart, and Chinese laborers carried the pieces to the valley side of the construction, where the stage was reassembled. The tourists enjoyed the novelty of the experience. Today's Wawona Road parallels the original road closely and connects with Highway 41 at the park boundary. In the early days, it took a full day's travel from Yosemite Valley to Wawona, with three changes of horses en route. Your trip today will take about an hour.

W-1 BRIDALVEIL FALL

You may enjoy a nearby view of Bridalveil Fall from the parking area here, or an even more intimate experience awaits just a quarter of a mile up a paved path. The local American Indians said there was a bad spirit in these waters. Legend has it that Pohono, an evil, puffing wind spirit, would take people who got too close to the waterfall. Those taken would be held prisoner in the waters until they took another in turn.

There is a wind phenomenon associated with this waterfall. In the afternoon, especially during the summer, an up-canyon wind slams into the cliff and continues upward, causing water at the top of the fall to blow backward upon itself. At times, the wind is strong enough to hold back the entire flow until it suddenly gushes forth, only to be blocked once again.

At night, the air over the mountains cools and flows back down the creek, tumbling over the cliff in an air-fall. When it hits the valley floor, local-

A storm clears, revealing the cliffs and waterfalls of Yosemite Valley from **W-2**.

ized winds tear through the forests and woodlands, tossing the crowns of trees wildly. The wind is localized to a few acres near the bottom of the fall. It can be spooky.

It is, in fact, dangerous near the fall. People have died there. Is Pohono responsible? No one knows for sure, but be sure to stay on the path, and do not climb above the viewing area.

The view of Bridalveil Fall from the viewing area is intimate and often wet.

W-1 to W-2 is 1.5 miles. W-2 will be on your right.

W-2 TUNNEL VIEW

Imagine yourself among the first outsiders to see Yosemite Valley. When the Mariposa Battalion first entered Yosemite Valley on March 27, 1851, Lafayette Bunnell was so taken by the view that he stopped to take it all in. Later he wrote of his experience:

Haze hung over the valley—light as gossamer—and clouds partially dimmed the higher cliffs and mountains. This obscurity of vision but increased the awe with which I beheld it, and as I looked, a peculiar exalted sensation seemed to fill my whole being, and I found my eyes in tears with emotion.

LAFAYETTE BUNNELL,
DISCOVERY OF THE YOSEMITE

The other men were mostly concerned about Indians and didn't see the beauty as Lafayette Bunnell had. One man later said that if he had known the Valley was going to become famous, he would have looked. Today we don't have to concern ourselves with enemy distractions. Take the time to allow the power of this view to work its magic on you.

W-2 to W-3 is 5.2 miles. W-3 will be on your right.

W-3 THE A-ROCK FIRE COMPLEX

On August 7, 1990, at about 2:00 p.m., lightning started a wildfire that was spotted an hour later near Steamboat Bay on the Merced River below. Air tankers arrived on scene within 2 hours and began dropping fire retardant. Another fire, the A-Rock Fire, was spotted, and firefighters went there. Ultimately, the two fires grew and were fought as one, which took the name the A-Rock Complex.

Even though these fires were aggressively fought, they grew rapidly, and on August 10, all roads leading to Yosemite Valley were closed. The fire roared up the canyon through here, changing the scene from coniferous forest to the shrubby landscape we see today.

We are seeing larger and larger fires in the Sierra and the West. Many decades of fire suppression have allowed forests to grow thick with fuels, from forest litter to multiple generations of conifers growing in thickets.

The purpose of Yosemite National Park is to preserve nature in as pristine a condition as possible. Lightning-caused fire is as much a part of the forest ecosystem as rain or snow, and the National Park Service knows fire needs to be restored to its natural place in Yosemite. With this in mind, fire crews purposefully set fires under rigorous prescriptions to reduce fuels and return Yosemite's vegetation to a more natural state.

For more on the A-Rock Fire Complex, see under **B-4** on page 52.

W-3 to W-4 is 2.4 miles. W-4 will be on your left.

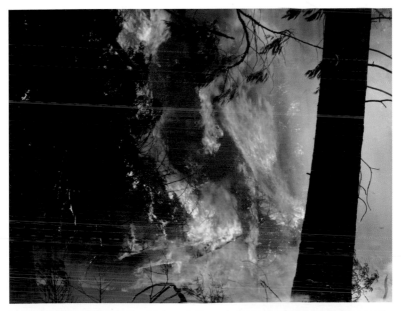

The A-Rock Fire of 1990 burned intensely through dense, dry forest in the lower and upper montane zones.

Chinquapin, a common shrub found at the top of the lower montane forest, gives its name to the location of W-4.

W-4 CHINQUAPIN

Chinquapin is where the Glacier Point Road branches off to Badger Pass and Glacier Point (for more on Chinquapin, see page 99). If you are going to drive up the Glacier Point Road, stop in the parking area and read the introduction to this road on page 105.

Yosemite West

Yosemite West, .5 miles south of Chinquapin, is a private community just outside the national park boundary.

W-4 to W-5 is 11.0 miles. W-5 will be on your right.

W-5 WAWONA CAMPGROUND

When the national park was created in 1890, there was no National Park Service to protect the new parklands. The following year, the U.S. Cavalry began administering the park on a seasonal basis, from about mid-May to October. The first administration site was Camp A. E. Wood (after Captain Ahram Epperson Wood), which stood on the site of today's Wawona Campground.

W-5 to W-6 is 1.0 mile. W-6 will be on your left.

W-6 PIONEER YOSEMITE HISTORY CENTER

The Pioneer Yosemite History Center is an assemblage of buildings from around Yosemite that are symbolic of various eras in the history of Yosemite National Park. For example, George Anderson's cabin is a portal

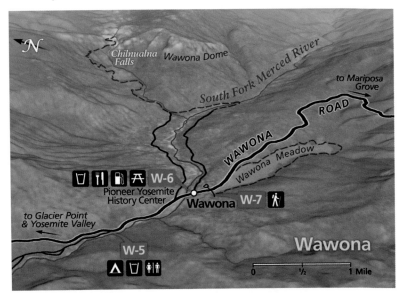

The past comes alive on a California mud wagon at the Pioneer Yosemite History Center. Stage driver Burl "Buckshot" Maier interprets early travel in Yosemite.

to the 1870s, when this blacksmith and entrepreneur made the first ascent of Half Dome and began work on a road toward its top. He had planned to charge tolls as well as build a hotel at the base of the climb.

Another building, the U.S. Cavalry Office of the Acting Superintendent, transports visitors to the early years of the national parks, before the National Park Service, when the cavalry cared for these precious lands.

A number of vintage wagons and carriages from Yosemite's past are also displayed for you to see. Contemplate how your visit to the park might have differed if at a time before automobiles. Your visit may be enlivened by a short tour on a California mud wagon—typical transportation used to get to Yosemite Valley in the nineteenth and early twentieth century; tours are often available during the summer season.

W-6 to W-7 is 0.6 mile. T-7 will be on your right.

W-7 WAWONA MEADOW

Meadows in Yosemite haven't always been protected as wild, natural, and free from the effects of human use. The Wawona Meadow is no different. Over the years, it was heavily grazed by horses and cattle; such use caused a change in plant communities.

The southern end was used as an airstrip until the late 1930s, and the golf course, built in 1918, continues to be used today. In an attempt to dry the meadow, the Civilian Conservation Corps (CCC) dug two-mile-long ditches to divert water to the meadow's edge.

While grazing in the meadow stopped in 1970, we have been left with 165 acres of greatly changed parklands. Some of the CCC ditches had widened and deepened as much as ten feet in places through erosion. The meadow no longer supported many of the native plant communities that once grew there, and

Wawona Meadow restoration. *Upper left:* 2009—A six- to eight-foot-deep ditch here shows typical erosion. *Upper right:* 2010—After filling in the ditch, restoration workers spread erosion control blankets, then cover them with woody debris. *Lower left:* 2011—After one winter, additional sediment and woody debris have moved in over the filled-in area. *Lower right:* 2012—After two winters, plant recovery is well underway.

invasive non-native species were taking hold.

In 2010, Yosemite's restoration ecologists began work to bring the meadow back to its natural state. Since the CCC ditches had dried the meadow and lowered the ground-water considerably, crews hauled in thousands of cubic yards of soil to fill in the ditches and restore the meadow topography.

Restoration crews replanted salvaged vegetation, seeded areas with locally gathered seeds, and planted plugs of sedge taken from nearby. The water table rose, and the meadow is on its way to becoming the meadow it once was, supporting habitat for plants and animals, including several rare and sensitive species.

You can explore the Wawona Meadow on a practically level 3.5-mile loop that will take about 2 hours to walk.

Begin at the Wawona Hotel and walk across the golf course on the paved road. Once across the golf course, take the first left onto the unpaved fire road that loops around the meadow.

W-7 to W-8 is 4.1 miles. W-8 will be on the right. There is no place to park until you pass the entrance station, so read the following before you set off.

W-8 SOUTH ENTRANCE / MARIPOSA GROVE OF GIANT SEQUOIAS

At the stop sign, those who wish to exit the park will turn to the right and pass through the South Entrance of Yosemite National Park. If you want to visit the Mariposa Grove, drive straight ahead from the stop sign. The road will end in the grove of giant sequoias.

During the late spring, summer, and early fall, you may need to take the free shuttle bus to get to the Mariposa Grove if the small parking lot is full. If this is the case, go back to the parking area near the gas station in Wawona and board the next shuttle. In winter, the road is usually closed by snow.

The Mariposa Grove is part of the original grant that protected Yosemite Valley and the giant sequoias in 1864. There is a self-guiding trail from the parking area to the Grizzly Giant, one of the largest trees in the grove. Brochures are available at the beginning of the trail, and informative signs along the way explain some of the ecology of these venerable trees.

For information on giant sequoias, see the following section.

GIANT SEQUOIAS

There are three groves of giant sequoias in Yosemite National Park: the Mariposa Grove, the Merced Grove, and the Tuolumne Grove. The largest and most accessible is the Mariposa Grove, which is 4.3 miles from the South Entrance to Yosemite National Park.

Giants in the Mist

There was once a time when moist forests dominated many landscapes on planet Earth. It was a time when sequoia trees and their relatives flourished. We know this because their fossils have been found throughout North America, Europe, and Asia. Scientists have even unearthed fossils of an extinct giant sequoia in the deserts of Nevada.

Three species of sequoia trees survive today. One, the dawn redwood (*Metasequoia glyptostroboides*), grows in a single valley in China. Another, the coast redwood (*Sequoia sempervirens*), lives on the California coast from about 100 miles south of San Francisco and north to just across the Oregon border. The third, the giant sequoia (*Sequoiadendron giganteum*), only grows naturally on the west slope of the Sierra Nevada of California.

Giant sequoias in the Mariposa Grove during a thunderstorm.

These descendants of a long line of moisture-loving plants have evolved with the land and climate to exist in their limited ranges today. Interestingly, many of these three types of sequoias have been planted around the world and do grow well.

Forty-eight giant sequoias that were planted in Yosemite Valley survive today, the largest of which is on the grounds of the Ahwahnee Hotel. There is also a coast redwood growing in back of the Yosemite Museum, where it was planted as a specimen of its species to be compared with the giant sequoia.

What happened? Why did the sequoia trees die out? Why do they live naturally only in a few places today? The answer has to do with past climate change. Places where *Sequoiadendron chaneyi* once grew in Nevada are now in desert landscapes that receive less than half the precipitation there once was.

If we could see the last 100 million years of Earth's history like a time-lapse movie, we would see vegetation patterns moving about, coming and going on the land as continents separated and mountains grew. Toward the end of the movie, we would see a verdant Nevada dry up and become desert as the Sierra Nevada rose, cutting moisture off from the west. Conditions favorable to sequoia trees would be gone.

Giant sequoias have been known to science for a century and a half for their massive, awe-inspiring beauty—beauty that inspired the idea of protecting nature in parks and further inspired the creation of national parks throughout the world.

Most giant sequoias live in about seventy groves concentrated mostly in Sequoia and Kings Canyon National Parks and Sequoia National Monument on the western slope of the southern Sierra Nevada. The grove count varies because some groves are so close together that they are sometimes counted as one.

There are only eight widely separated groves between the Kings River and the northernmost grove. Three of those groves are in Yosemite. What is it about these locations that allows giant sequoias to survive, and why are they so widely spaced in the north? No single answer has been discovered.

Giant sequoias are found in a Mediterranean climate characterized by dry summers. Mean annual precipitation in the groves varies from about 35 to 55 inches, with considerable variation from year to year.

Most of this precipitation falls primarily as snow during fall, winter, and early spring, when cross-country skiers enjoy as much as 6 feet on the ground. Because so little rain falls

Dawn redwood, redwood, and giant sequoia cones (not to scale).

Even once they have fallen, giant sequoias take a very long time to decay.

during the summer months, these huge trees must grow where there is ample groundwater. Some studies indicate giant sequoia grove locations may be related to underground streams.

The upper elevation limit for these trees seems to be related to exceptionally low temperatures, while soil moisture appears to control the lower limit. Although seedlings do not survive in wet soils, adequate soil moisture throughout the dry growing season is critical for successful establishment of giant sequoias from seedlings to adults.

Giant Sequoias and Fire

Fire may cause the most serious damage to giant sequoias, and yet, ironically, fire is the most important factor for the survival of these venerable trees. Even though a mature giant sequoia resists fire with its thick, nonresinous bark and high crown, it, too, can eventually succumb. Century after century, fires repeatedly burn through the bark, killing living tissues and producing fire scars.

If you observe the largest trees in a grove, you'll find fire scars on most. This is what gives individual character to such trees as the Grizzly Giant,

the Clothespin Tree, and the Telescope Tree. While few mature giants are killed directly by fire, the loss of supporting wood does predispose them to falling. In addition, fire scars appear to be the main cause of dead tops, so common in older trees.

Fire can kill seedlings and saplings, but frequent light fire creates seedbeds with exposed mineral soil and well-lighted openings in the canopy that are most favorable for successful germination and early growth of giant sequoia seedlings. Fuels in these places tend to be sparser and to accumulate more slowly than in adjacent forested areas. The more vigorous seedlings and saplings can get to be large enough to survive the next fire by the time it occurs.

The most significant impact of humans on giant sequoia groves has been fire suppression. Damage caused by fire is outweighed by its benefits in perpetuating the species. Furthermore, the elimination of frequent fires has permitted large buildups of both dead and live fuels. This buildup increases the potential for catastrophic crown fires. The National Park Service has well-researched and carefully planned programs designed to reintroduce fire into giant sequoia ecosystems.

Lottery Tickets for a Giant

Some say each giant sequoia seed has one chance in a million to become a mature tree.

Unlike most pines, which lose their cones soon after they mature, giant sequoia cones may remain green on the tree and are viable for more than 20 years. A single tree may hold as many as 10,000 to 30,000 cones at any one time.

There are three ways cones dry out and release their seeds. The most important is probably fire. This is because moderate- to high-intensity fire dries the cones, which then release tens of thousands of seeds.

The other two ways involve animals: One is an insect, and the other is a mammal.

The insect is a longhorn wood-boring beetle (*Phymatodes nitidus*). The larvae of this beetle eat their way through the cone, often damaging the vasculature tissue, and the cone dries. As it dries, the cone scales shrink, allowing the seeds to fall.

Any observant person can learn the identity of the mammal by sitting long enough beneath a giant sequoia. Eventually the sound of something rushing through the air is followed by a thud. If you look carefully, you'll find that it was a sequoia cone. Look up, and you may see a tiny squirrel high in the trees.

This smallish tree squirrel, called a chickaree, or Douglas squirrel, scampers up these mammoth tree trunks like a lizard on a barn wall. Then, high in the crowns of these huge trees, the squirrel chews through the stems of the green cones, and down they fall. The chickaree eats the fleshy part of the cone and leaves the stem and central part. Some people call these leavings "cone cobs."

The seeds are so inconsequential—about the size of a flake of oatmeal—that squirrels don't pay much attention to them, and they are allowed to flutter to the ground. Douglas squirrels are active year round and store a considerable number of cones in caches hidden about the forests. Squirrels forget some of these secret

A low-intensity fire burns undergrowth in the Mariposa Grove.

The museum in the Mariposa Grove gives scale to these mammoth trees.

pantries, and the cones eventually dry and release their seeds.

Each giant sequoia cone contains 200 seeds, and mature trees bear an average of 1,500 cones in a year. That's 300,000 seeds per year. If each giant were to replace itself every 1,500 years, it would have produced nearly 500 million seeds. At that rate, surely the odds are greater than one in a million for a particular seed to become a mature tree. The rare beauty of a giant sequoia is indeed a very special thing.

Symbols of America's National Parks

If you were to visit any National Park Service area—be it Yellowstone National Park, Women's Rights National Historical Park, or the Washington Monument—you would find images of giant sequoias on the rangers' uniforms. The hatband (illustrated below) is embossed with giant sequoia foliage and cones. It has two gold cones on the left side. The official National Park Service belt also has giant sequoia cones and foliage embossed on it. The large green tree on the shoulder patch is a giant sequoia.

Set aside in 1890 as national parks, Yosemite, General Grant (now Kings Canyon), and Sequoia National Parks preserve giant sequoias. They were three of the earliest national parks in existence. While Yellowstone was set aside as the first national park in 1872, the Yosemite Grant of 1864, which included the Mariposa Grove, provided the seed of an idea that led to our national park system, as well as preserves throughout the world.

All National Park Service hatbands are embossed with giant sequoia cones and foliage and decorated with golden cones on the side.

Tenaya Canyon

Half Dome

Mt. Starr King

Nevada Fall

Vernal Fall

Illilouette Creek

Glacier Point

G-7

G-6

Yosemite Village

Illilouette Fall

Yosemite Falls

Sentinel Dome

G-8

Taft Point

G-5

Bridalveil Creek

ROAD

G-9

Bridalveil Creek

G-4

Bridalveil Fall

POINT

G-3

Glacier Point Road closed late fall–late spring east of Badger Pass

Badger Pass

G-2

YOSEMITE NATIONAL PARK

Yosemite Valley

GLACIER

G-1

G-10

to Wawona

Chinquapin

WAWONA

to Crane Flat

Merced River

ROAD

to Wawona

Arch Rock Entrance

Yosemite West

SIERRA N.F.

Foresta

N

0   1   2 Miles

to El Portal

Glacier Point Road

Glacier Point Road

16.2

Travelers who go to Glacier Point must return via the same road. Therefore, there are marker posts on the way out and different ones on the way back. The Glacier Point Road, which originally struck off from the Wawona Road near the restrooms at Chinquapin (see **W-4** on page 86), was completed in 1882 at a cost of $8,000. It was part of a road system conceived and built by the Yosemite Stage & Turnpike Company, owned by Albert Henry Washburn and his brothers. Like other road builders, they saw possible profit in charging tolls. Beyond that, they also felt that a good road with access to the Mariposa Grove and Glacier Point would bring back tourists lost to the two new toll roads into Yosemite Valley on the north side of the river. The new road parallels the old road closely.

At about 6,000 feet elevation, Chinquapin is near the top of the lower montane forest with its mix of white fir, ponderosa pine, incense-cedar, sugar pine, and black oak. Chinquapin gets its name from the com-

mon shrub that grows here, called chinquapin. The road winds through the upper montane zone and slightly into the subalpine zone. (For more on Yosemite's life zones, see pages 18–19.) Several flowery meadows lie near the road along the way. Watch for bears and other wildlife crossing the road.

The destination of the road in the summer season is Glacier Point, with its spectacular views into Yosemite Valley, over a half mile below, as well as Half Dome and dozens of High Sierra peaks. In winter, road crews plow the road only to the Badger Pass ski area.

W-4 to G-1 is 2.2 miles. G-1 will be on your right.

G-1 WHITE FIR

Two large white fir trees encrusted with chartreuse lichens stand at either end of this turnout. The one at the upper end is near a pair of red fir trees. Look up at the two and compare their foliage.

Glacier Point Road.

easily. The red fir is a member of the upper montane zone.

Here, where the two meet, is a transitional area between the upper and lower montane zones. As you continue up in elevation, you may notice more and more red fir trees.

A common animal here is the chickaree, or Douglas squirrel. Gray squirrels are more common at lower elevations. Northern flying squirrels are also quite common, but they work the night shift and are difficult to see. Black bears roam these forests, especially near meadows, where they love to eat grasses and wildflowers in the spring.

The bright yellow-green lichens growing on the bark of these trees are called wolf lichen because it contains a component of a poison used in Europe to kill wolves. Lichen is an association of two organisms that grow together. One is a fungus and the other is an algae. The fungus provides structure, and the algae provide sugar through photosynthesis. They don't hurt the trees; they just use them for a place to grow.

The white fir may seem fuller because its needles grow outward from the branches, while the red fir needles tend to bend upward from their branches. Another way to discern one from the other is that red fir needles are squarish in cross section and roll easily between forefinger and thumb, while the white fir needles are flat and don't roll so

Chipped bark reveals the inner colors of red fir (*left*) and white fir (*right*).

G-1 to **G-2** is 2.7 miles. **G-2** will be on your right.

G-2 BADGER PASS

Badger Pass was the first established ski area in California. Technically, the location of Badger Pass is about 0.25 mile east of the ski lodge. It's at a high point along the old Glacier Point wagon road. In the early days, people used the area near the pass as a place to ski. Eventually the lodge was built at its present location on the north edge of Monroe Meadow, and ski runs were developed on the slopes south of the lodge.

Monroe Meadow bears the name of one of the wagon drivers who carried passengers to and from Glacier Point, as well as on other routes to and from Yosemite. He worked for Henry Washburn, who had this to say about him:

After an experience of nearly forty years, and having had as many as fifty regular drivers some season, I have never known another such an all-round reinsman as George Monroe. Just as there are the greatest of soldiers and sailors, . . . so there are greater stage drivers than their fellows—and George Monroe was the greatest of all.

He was a wonder in every way. He had names for all his horses, and they all knew their names. . . . He seldom or never used the whip, except to crack it over their heads. . . .

He drove over my lines for nearly twenty years and never injured a person. I always put him on the box when there was a distinguished party to be driven, and fast and showy driving was expected or necessary, and he never disappointed me or exceeded the limit scheduled or fell behind.

Once he drove a party from the valley to Madera, a distance of seventy miles,

in eleven hours, and in two hours afterward, in an emergency, took the reins and drove back to Wawona.

Once, coming down the last grade into Mariposa, his brake broke short off while his teams were on a clean run and he dashed the whole outfit into a chaparral clump; in less than two hours he had the animals extricated, the stage pulled out, and was trotting into Mariposa; he came into Merced on time; the fourteen passengers made up a purse of seventy dollars for him, and the two English ladies aboard sent him acceptable Christmas presents annually until I informed them of his death some years later. . . .

Thousands of people have telegraphed to reserve seats on his stage or have staid over at Wawona to drive with him.

As described by Washburn, such was the case when President Ulysses S. Grant and his family visited Yosemite.

[Monroe] sat there, with his six lines and long whip, with one foot on the brake and the other braced against the footboard. . . . He would throw those six animals from one side to the other to avoid a stone or a chuck

George Monroe.

*hole as if they were a machine or a
single quadruped; sometimes a hub
would just gently scrape the bank
on the upper side, and in a moment
afterward infinitesimally overlap the
precipice on the down side. Crack!
went his whip, every once in a while,
and down would go the teams on a
rapturous canter, and around the
sharp curves and over plank culverts,
and up again on a clean run.*

"THE PASSING OF A SIERRA KNIGHT,"
OVERLAND MONTHLY, JULY 1903

Monroe drove for Presidents Hayes
and Garfield as well. Whenever there
was an important or famous person
to be driven, George was at the reins.

**G-2 to G-3 is 1.0 mile. G-3 will be on
your right.**

G-3 SUMMIT MEADOW

Meadows cover only 3 percent of the
total area of Yosemite National Park,
yet as many as a third of the park's
plant species grow in them. Typical
of upper montane meadows, Summit Meadow has a wide variety of
plant species. Jeffrey's shooting star,
blue camas, western bistort, corn
lily, Macloskey's violet, and western
dog violet are a few of the many
wildflowers that brighten Summit
Meadow in the summer.

**G-3 to G-4 is 2.7 miles. G-4 will be
on your right.**

G-4 BRIDALVEIL CREEK CAMPGROUND

If you ever think life was easier in the
past, consider the story of Charles
and Mary Agnes Peregoy. Born in
Baltimore, Charles Peregoy caught
gold fever at the age of twenty-two
and headed for California in 1849.
After mining in various places in the
foothills of the Sierra, he eventually
found himself in Mariposa, where he
purchased a ranch about two miles
south of town.

Shortly after Peregoy made the
final payment on the ranch, John C.
Frémont claimed the land as part of
his Mexican land grant and insisted
that Peregoy pay him rent. Peregoy
refused to pay and brought the matter to court. The legal battle dragged
on and on.

Meanwhile, rather than put money
into the ranch only to lose it, Charles
Peregoy began raising cattle. During
the summers, he took them to a
high mountain meadow, where he,
his wife, and five children lived. The
meadow sat along the horse and foot
trail about halfway between Clark's
Station (Wawona) and Yosemite
Valley, and came to be called Peregoy
Meadow.

When tourists began stopping and
asking for food and lodging, Charles
and his wife, Mary, built a small
inn they called the Mountain View
House. They themselves felled the
trees and assembled them into a log
structure that housed an office, a
kitchen, a dining room, and accommodations for sixteen guests.

Mountain View House opened
in 1869. Later the Peregoys built
another structure that served
as a living room and additional
accommodations.

Six years later, in 1875, the Wawona
wagon road opened, drawing traffic
away from the old horse trail. Fewer
and fewer parties stopped by, the
Mountain View House fell into disuse, and Charles and Mary moved
away.

You are alongside the meadow where
the Peregoys had their cattle camp
and built the Mountain View House.
By the way, the court case regard-

ing Charles Peregoy's ranch went on for seventeen years. It was finally decided in his favor.

G-4 to G-5 is 2.8 miles. G-5 will be on your right.

G-5 CLARK RANGE VIEW

After his wife died of consumption (known today as tuberculosis), Galen Clark placed his children with their aunts and uncles and headed west. He eventually found himself in the Mariposa area.

When in 1853, at the age of thirty-nine, he began to develop symptoms similar to his deceased wife, he went to a doctor, who confirmed his fears. He had consumption. Imagine what he must have thought facing the same disease that had killed his wife. What would you do in those days when tuberculosis was considered incurable?

Clark, who had recently been part of the second tourist party to enter Yosemite Valley, thought, "If I'm to die, I want to live out the last days of my life in the most beautiful place I have ever seen," so in 1857,

he moved to the Yosemite area and waited to die.

Of course, he had to provide for his basic needs while he waited, so he built a small cabin in the meadowlands of Wawona. He hunted game and explored the mountains. On one of his hunts, he and Albert Henry Washburn (see **G-6** on page 105) came across the Mariposa Grove, which he named.

More tourists visited Yosemite and the Mariposa Grove, and Clark's place in Wawona turned out to be perfect for people to stop over on their journey from the town of Mariposa to Yosemite Valley. Clark offered hospitalities and extolled the wonders of his beloved Mariposa giant sequoias.

While he waited to die, Clark witnessed the creation of America's first scenic park. Given to California by the federal government to be administered essentially as a state park, it was called the Yosemite Grant and included Yosemite Valley and the Mariposa Grove. Clark was appointed guardian of the new park. As such, he made improvements

Mount Starr King   Mount Clark   Gray Peak   Red Peak   Merced Peak

Clark Range.

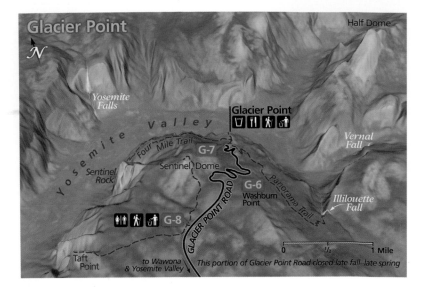

Half Dome

Yosemite Falls

Glacier Point

Yosemite Valley

Four Mile Trail

G-7

Sentinel Dome

Yosemite

Sentinel Rock

GLACIER POINT ROAD

G-6

Washburn Point

Panorama Trail

Vernal Fall

Illilouette Fall

G-8

Taft Point

to Wawona & Yosemite Valley

0   ½   1 Mile

This portion of Glacier Point Road closed late fall–late spring

to the valley and showed people through his beloved giant sequoias, where he built a log shelter.

Still waiting to die, Clark dug his own grave in Yosemite Valley and planted giant sequoia seedlings there to surround him in his everlasting sleep. Giant sequoias require frequent watering when they are young, so Clark had to dig a well nearby. Imagine someone asking a local, "Can you tell me where I might find Galen Clark?" and hearing the answer, "I believe he is over at the cemetery watering his grave."

Galen Clark.

While he was waiting to die, Clark wrote a Yosemite guidebook, another about the Indian people he had befriended, and a third about his beloved giant sequoias.

Changes in state politics temporarily ended Clark's guardianship when a new board of governors for the park brought in their own appointee. Later, Clark was called back into service as guardian of Yosemite, where he worked for another eight years. He finally retired from the post but continued on in Yosemite working as a guide.

Galen Clark was thirty-nine when he found out he had consumption and forty-two when he moved to Yosemite. In those days, a man his age, in good health, could not expect to live beyond his sixties. Clark finally died a few days before his ninety-sixth birthday!

If you would like to spend a couple of hours hiking, there is a parking area on the left side of the road between the Clark Range viewpoint and Washburn Point. See **G-8** on page 106, for descriptions.

G-5 to G-6 is 4.3 miles. G-6 will be on your right.

G-6 WASHBURN POINT

Albert Henry Washburn ran the Yosemite Stage & Turnpike Company, beginning in 1879. This company built the original Wawona Road as well as the original Glacier Point Road. Some say the views from Washburn Point rival the views from Glacier Point—perhaps they even exceed them.

Jeffrey pines—large pine trees with bark like alligator skin and needles in bundles of three—are typical of dry slopes within the upper montane zone. A similar species, the ponderosa pine, lives in the lower montane zone. The Jeffrey pine can be identified by its smell—it has a sweet odor. Try it yourself: put your nose inside one of the large cracks in one of the trees and breathe deeply. Some smell like vanilla; others like butterscotch. What do you smell?

G-6 to G-7 is 0.7 mile. G-7 will be at the parking area at the end of the road.

G-7 GLACIER POINT

No one knows when Glacier Point got its name, but it was in use as early as 1864, the year the Yosemite Grant was signed by Abraham Lincoln. Another mystery is how the name came about. There is no vista of a glacier, and at the time people thought a cataclysmic earthquake created Yosemite, not glaciers.

The mystery of how Glacier Point got its name will probably remain unanswered. We now know that glaciers have flowed past Glacier Point many times in the last 2 million years.

There is a short, pleasant walk to Glacier Point from the parking area. Along the way, you may take in several views of the high country to the east. One is from a stone hut,

View from Washburn Point of Mount Starr King with Clark Range in the background.

Mount Hoffmann
North Dome
Basket Dome
Mount Watkins
Tenaya Peak
Echo Peaks
Clouds Rest
Half Dome
Vogelsang Peak
Mount Broderick

View from Glacier Point.

where you may learn more of the geologic story. There is a wheelchair-accessible route to Glacier Point from the parking area.

A steep hike (but a short one) leads to nearby Illilouette Fall, a gorgeous waterfall that relatively few people see. Some hikers like to continue along the Panorama Cliff to the top of Nevada Fall, and then into Yosemite Valley via Vernal Fall. The total trip to Yosemite Valley via these trails is about 8.5 miles. If you would like to take a shorter walk to the floor of Yosemite Valley, try the Four Mile Trail. It was about 4 miles long when it was originally opened in 1872, but with repairs and additions over the years, the distance now is 4.8 miles.

G-7 to G-8 is 2.3 miles. G-8 will be on your right.

G-8 SENTINEL DOME / TAFT POINT TRAILHEAD

Sentinel Dome was named after Sentinel Rock, which was named for its fancied likeness to a huge watch-tower, as seen from Yosemite Valley. The dome is 8,122 feet above sea level, nearly as high as Half Dome.

William Howard Taft, the twenty-seventh president of the United States, first visited Yosemite in the autumn of 1909. Legend has it that Taft, a rather large man, felt sorry for his horse on the trip down the Four Mile Trail to Yosemite Valley, so he walked the distance, leading his horse down the steep trail.

There is an easy 1.1-mile trail to Taft Point that begins right here. Another easy 1.1-mile trail leads from here to the top of Sentinel Dome. Either trail is highly rewarding; both end at locations with extraordinary views. There is also a trail that connects Sentinel

Mount Florence

Mount Clark

Liberty Cap

Nevada Fall

Vernal Fall

granites in Yosemite. It's as though the mountains are made up of layers, like the layers in an onion, and as those layers are peeled back by erosion, they turn some mountains into domes. Such is the case with Sentinel Dome.

G-8 to G-9 is 5.1 miles. G-9 will be on your right.

G-9 BRIDALVEIL CREEK

This creek flows over the 620-foot-high cliff at Bridalveil Fall throughout the year. By contrast, Yosemite Falls dry up by the end of most summers. Why the difference?

The soils in this watershed are deeper and more developed than those of Yosemite Creek. Deeper soil means more groundwater, plus there are more meadows that slow the discharge of surface water. Also, the drainage for Bridalveil Creek tends to be more north facing, while Yosemite Creek's drainage has mostly southern exposure.

G-9 to G-10 is 5.6 miles. G-10 will be on your right.

Dome with Taft Point, providing an opportunity for a loop of 4.8 miles.

Across the street in the road cut, you may have noticed that the granite is cracked roughly parallel to the surface of the landscape. This is typical of some of the more massive

A trail to the top of Sentinel Dome rewards hikers with a 360 degree view of Yosemite.

View of Merced Canyon, Sierra foothills, and the Coast Range in the distance.

G-10 MERCED CANYON VIEW

This is one of the best places in Yosemite to watch the sun dip below the horizon. Often, in winter, fog in California's Central Valley creeps into the foothills below, creating a sublime sight as the sun sets behind the Coast Range more than 100 miles in the distance. Look for Mount Diablo near the San Francisco Bay Area. It will appear as a rounded double mountain near the far right of the Coast Range if the air is clear enough.

From here you can also see the Merced Gorge below, where the Merced River snakes its way west through the foothills to the flat plains of the Central Valley. There it joins the San Joaquin River, and the waters from Yosemite flow to San Francisco Bay and out through the Golden Gate to the Pacific Ocean. Eventually they will evaporate and ride the winds back to the Sierra to fall as snow and rain, and begin their long journey back to the sea.

ACKNOWLEDGMENTS

I would like to acknowledge those who helped me in some way on this project. In alphabetical order: Gwenyth Barrow, Sue Beatty, Monica Buhler, Les Chow, Ben Cunningham-Summerfield, Linda Eade, Margaret Eissler, Travis Espinosa, Dave Humphrey, Emily Jacobs, Jennifer Jacobs, Mary Kline, Caitlin Lee-Roney, Tom Medema, Peggy Moore, Dean Shenk, Greg Stock, Steve Thompson, Jeffrey Trust, and Gary Wuchner.

Index

YOSEMITE
CONSERVANCY.

Providing For Yosemite's Future

Yosemite Conservancy is the only philanthropic organization dedicated exclusively to the protection and preservation of Yosemite National Park and enhancement of the visitor experience. The Conservancy works to restore trails and protect wildlife through scientific research and habitat restoration, and offers outdoor programs that provide visitors with unique ways to connect with the park. It has funded projects in areas including trail and habitat restoration, wildlife protection, education, volunteering, and the production of award-winning books and DVDs.